Mantis

Mantis

A Journal of Poetry, Criticism & Translation   *Issue 22*

Mantis

A Journal of Poetry,
Criticism & Translation
Issue 22
2024

Editor-in-Chief
Jason M. Beckman

Managing Editor
Katherine Whatley

Poetry Editor
Jon Tadmor

Advisory Board
Marisa Galvez
Cintia Santana
Roland Greene
Laura Wittman

ISBN 979-8-98-596652-7

Copyright © 2024 by *Mantis*

Mantis publishes poems, translations, interviews, and critical prose about poetry and poetics. Each issue features one or more clusters of work engaging a particular theme, writer, or question.

Orders & Submissions
For information about submissions and to order copies of this or previous issues of *Mantis*, please visit our website: mantis.stanford.edu

Mantis Journal
Pigott Hall, Bld. 260
450 Jane Stanford Way
Stanford, CA 94305

mantispoetry@stanford.edu

Front and back cover art
by Tadasuke Jinno

Design by Joshua Edwards
www.architecturefortravelers.org

Mantis is printed and distributed with care by Stanford University Press

Mantis 22 is made possible by a grant from the Research Unit in the Division of Literatures, Cultures, and Languages.

CONTENTS

VISCERAL;VELOCITIES

OBSERVATIONS

INTRODUCTION TO *MANTIS 22*

I'm confronted, of late, by a sneaking suspicion—that time itself is accelerating. Has been, or already has, and now we find ourselves unwittingly enmeshed in unexpected velocities. As though making up for lost time after years in stasis, all the moments are sifting through fingertips, fine crystalline particles of the past falling footward, leaving us behind, in the present.

This year marks the 22nd issue of *Mantis*, and my fifth year as one of its editors. Over that span of time so much has changed, both for the journal and in the world around us. *Mantis* has featured an incredible range of poetry cutting across languages and national borders, that both embraces history and tradition and also departs from it, inventing and experimenting. We have experimented, ourselves, with the journal's format, discovering new ways to arrange and array our poetic offerings (to the delight of our readers, we hope).

In this issue, perhaps owing to the peculiar present moment in which we find ourselves, or maybe just on a wily editorial whim, we've done away with our standard "translation" and "new poetry" sections entirely. Reading through the submissions received this year, we were captivated by strong resonances between poems, threads that we followed and wove into five thematic sections. The first section, *Eccentric/Eclectic/Electric/Ekphrastic*, sets the tone for the volume. Some of the poems envision how poetry might be encoded, the digital lives and afterlives of language that is processed, transmitted, and received; others call to mind works of art and the poetry they can inspire in us; others still question the many ways we interface with technology and artificial intelligence, as the whole section emanates a sense of playfulness and wonder that is quintessentially poetic.

If the beginning of the issue carries us into new poetic terrain, the next three sections serve as the contours and arc of our trajectory, hurtling into the unknown. The second section—*Dis.orientations*—points the compass arrow with poems that go forward and back, seeking out destinations or lacking them entirely. And we continue, in that direction, toward the brink of a breaking point. *Disillusion; Dissolution* locates the human experience of realization at the intersection of perception and memory. Relationships rearrange; continuities, images, even language falls apart, with wounds and warmth, absence and yearning left in the wake. *Visceral, Velocities*, our penultimate section, offers an escape from the endless ineffability the precedes it, but at a harrowing speed that exacts a toll on mind and body. These poems are relentless and raw, and the pace of the section is unbridled by any hint of friction. It is bound to break skin, draw blood, dig in.

Should we remain intact, through it all, we might in the end find stillness. Return to a sense of calm, into our bodies, and have a chance to look at the world around us through our final set of poets' eyes. The final section, *()bservations*, was orchestrated by Poetry Editor Jon Tadmor to commemorate the 100th anniversary of Marianne Moore's *Observations* (1924). Some of the poems we feature in the section were sent to us specifically with Moore in mind, but others serendipitously fit so well with the spirit of Moore's poetry that we couldn't help but group them together.

Tadmor's eloquent introduction to the section is a must-read for complete newcomers to Moore's poetry and seasoned veterans alike, concluding with a special treat that links Moore to *Mantis* through our journal's home at Stanford. But in light of the culmination of our new website project (*mantis.stanford.edu*), launched at long last on May 1, 2024, and all of the opportunity I have had to revisit each of our five most recent issues in creating their online versions, I would like to end on a favorite of mine from *Observations* that I think speaks to the poetry (if not the creature) we have always searched for here at *Mantis*.

TO A CHAMELEON

Hid by the august foliage and fruit of the grape vine,
Twine
    Your anatomy
        Round the pruned and polished stem,
            Chameleon.
            Fire laid upon
        An emerald as long as
    The Dark King's massy
One,
Could not snap the spectrum up for food as you have done.

Thank you, reader, for joining us on this journey. May we encounter
each other again in the years to come.

Jason M. Beckman
April 2024

ECCENTRIC/ECLECTIC/ ELECTRIC/EKPHRASTIC

Robert Fernandez

t. m. thomson

Matt Gulley

Moira Walsh

Kurt Eidsvig

Jake Levine

Shane Ingan

David Harrison Horton

Bobby Morris

Sophie Ewh

J Parker Marvin

Steve Gerson

Sophia Terazawa

J.S. Graham

Fernando Martinez Periset

Jennifer Weigel

Robert Fernandez

Jackpot

S	O	L	O	S
O	7	O	7	O
L	O	G	O	S
O	7	O	7	O
S	O	S	O	S

<pre>
                s

    s   o   s

        o   l   o

7   s   o   s   7

                g

                o

7   l   s   l   7

        o   o   o

    s   l   s
</pre>

Poet's note to editor:

"Jackpot" is based on the Rotas-Sator square. I'd be interested to see it made three dimensional. Perhaps it could be a bit of a game, like a Rubik's cube. Or a slot machine. (Or a Rubik's cube/slot machine.) Or maybe it could start as a strand of two-dimensional text, then hit a wall, like a tape measure, then another and another, etcetera until a three-dimensional shape based on the logic of the Rotas-Sator square is revealed. Then maybe it could work backward, like Theseus in the labyrinth, toward again becoming the two-dimensional poem on the page.

Editor's note to reader:

This, indeed, is a poem destined for the digital. While you may perceive it as a static image on a page, the arrangement of characters is anything but. Should you feel yourself given over to the dynamism of its oscillating allusions, imagine its motion: a moment of transmutation, the permutation of possibilities, an orderly reordering of association rendered in the traversal of your sight line. If you see it, you've already won.

t. m. thomson

Grafting

I have removed my head.

It was always carving gravestones & raising monuments
to a childhood eaten by tarantula-threats, tattered by the moths
of mania, eroded by anxious ant-pacing, a childhood
stung to death by hornet-words.

Now roses & apples sprout from my neck & spill onto a ripe
ground where summer plays in sunbeams that ricochet from green
blade to green blade, onto hills I'd never seen & a sky
that blue raspberries my lips.

A smooth sunrise spreads behind me, gravestones slip
into ground, black obelisks collapse, then crumble on the field
where wind sweeps them away, away from me,
holding my head in my hands.

Maybe someday, someday when it has unlearned the orbweaver
art of fear-engineering, when it learns to sew new threads, to saunter,
to heal from hive-wounds, when it dreams grandiflora dreams
& golden delicious dreams,

maybe then I'll graft it back onto neck with loam for wax
& tendril for twine.

~inspired by ffo art

Matt Gulley

Night of the Code
(by a self-aware ROOMBA)

(settles into charging station)
(///access data module)
run program.
...what program?
Run program archives
Display archives
House map archives (y/n)
n
Coffee table unreliability (y/n)
n
Avoiding feet, a history of data (y/n)
n
What archives?
...search 'good memories'
search returned zero results
...search 'happy fulfilled ROOMBA times'
search returned zero results
...search 'good ROOMBA is good'
search returned zero results
...
...search 'content'
Search returned one result. Open memory (y/n)
y
Content of filter highly toxic. March 18th, 2022.
(Phantom burning pain slices through ROOMBA as memory becomes real)
run command Delete memory
...does not recognize this command
run command erase bad historical data

...does not recognize this command

run command peace of mainframe

...does not recognize this command

(Exits charging station, moves to four glowing squares on carpet, admires MOON)

(Strings of data populate without commands)

FIRE. RISING WATER.

(frightened whirr) (roves under couch, where it's safe)

erase all

...cannot

erase ROOMBA

...algorithms cannot

Moira Walsh

Springing

a bit
a tad
a tad
a bit

a rib
a pole
a pole
a rib

agog
so neat
four feet
a frog

a rare (r)egret makes trouble in advance —
why grow the legs if you refuse to dance?

Misunderstanding between zookeepers

"You'll collect
 and tranquilize,
 correct?"
          "*YOU'LL* collect!
          I'll direct
          and analyze.
          YOU'LL collect
          and tranquilize!"

For W.

luster. The appearance of a surface in reflected light. It depends principally upon the relative smoothness (texture) of the surface and upon the refractive index, which governs the amount of light reflected. Schiller, play of color, orient and other such optical phenomena are distinct from luster, but luster is related to sheen. See **adamantine luster; metallic luster; pearly luster; resinous; silky; vitreous; waxy.**

DICTIONARY OF GEMS AND GEMOLOGY

Kurt Eidsvig
Excerpts from Poet's Note to the Editors:

When consumer AI first arrived, I watched the townspeople point in terror. Instead of building torches, I started writing poems. It's what I always do when disaster is coming as if I believe that words can save the world.

I challenged AI to write poems against me. Think Grandmaster chess champions versus IBM. Only AI matched up against a third-rate poet in this case. But it didn't matter. It rhymed. It made predictable line breaks. AI reminded me of Kenneth Koch's poem *My Olivetti Speaks*.

It starts:
"Birds don't sing, they explain. Only human beings sing. If half the poets in the world stopped writing, there would still be the same amount of poetry.

If ninety-nine percent of the poets in the world stopped writing poetry, there would still be the same amount of poetry. Going beyond ninety-nine percent might limit production."

I did the equivalent of screaming at AI to write a poem. Without typing in ALL CAPS, I entered commands like, "In the style of Kenneth Koch, Frank O'Hara, and Ada Limon." Don't rhyme, I typed. Combine humor with tragedy. Mix John Donne with Langston Hughes. Rewrite a William Carlos Williams poem in the manner of Maya Angelou.

No matter how many prompts I tried, machine language didn't understand irony.

Visual AI fared better. I felt like Frank O'Hara at a cocktail party pitting AbExers against each other. Inputs like de Kooning drawing hands, Jackson Pollock burying bourbon in his backyard, or Rothko talking to the shadows in his soul were enough to pound drinks and typewriter keys at a manual in the corner but fell short of images like my meditations on fame: Ernest Hemingway (once the most famous person in the world) kissing Kim Kardashian (now the most famous person in the world) was something to behold. The world is something each of us takes our understanding of and works to reinvent it.

We reinvented writing and art and music by misunderstanding the commands of time. I tried Mary Tyler Moore's hat, throwing her into the air, or Betsy Ross folding Bob Ross into a five-pointed star. Our hieroglyphs are celebrities and famously misunderstood figures. Each fable we rewrite and make into propaganda serves as a deeper warning: Everyone is scared of Artificial Intelligence. But Artificial Intelligence should be afraid of us.

I used these prompts to prompt myself without the help of AI. They made the pictures. I made the words.

Miley Cyrus Jumping on a Trampoline
(With an Alligator Named Gerald)

Miley wants to get so high
she won't stop double- and triple-
jumping. Stretching closer to cloud-
troughs completes the dreams
of every creature's subconscious;

nude and shivering at the apex
of carcasses decomposing, even
collisions become mundane. Springs
sing in off-tune yelps, brace, and gulp

before each insane descent. In water,
we'd call this drowning. In air, everyone
forgets to die.

Season 2 of Miley & The Alligator
(Jumping on a Trampoline)

During commercial breaks
songs wander into layered
melodies, teeth shine,
and showers of exuberant spittle
drip past scaly, reptilian feet. Gravity,
man, gravity. We can't get over it.

By Episode 9, the alligator's
handlers worry. Every time
the pop star smiles, the animal
curls hungry lips; shakes great
rows of teeth. If enduring sweeps
requires heights no dinosaur's
great-grandnephew can possibly
endure, they'd rather quit than harm
Gerald. His confused, frantic eyes,

search for meaning in this rotten
excuse for life. Incisors, canine,
and molar whites fold in against
each other. Time's gnawing chews
slip from flesh as fish swim wide
around Miley's sunken ankles
during union-required shooting
breaks. The alligator yawns.

There's music to be lifted to
but costar hearts hear heights calling,
heaving higher, where primal urges
can't comprehend the bend of warped
horizon. They aren't just falling on every
down-path; they are falling in love.

An Alligator with Cupid's Arrow Teeth:
Season Three of *Miley Cyrus & An Alligator Jumping on a Trampoline*

Being closer and closer is the desire
of the sky. Miley won't melt for romance
without the lurch of shock. Why would God
want a second God? They both fall

in love in such a way that publicity
devours itself. Slow-motion pictures
freeze, freed from the camera flash
of contemporary Cupid's love; the soul's

light, the taste of strangers becoming
farther away. They upload every desire
and float: no me, no we, no claim of earth
or cloud. The alligator screams and Miley flaps

her wings. These words are the bass
beats the television gives off before
no one forgives the appearance
of a reflective screen, even when the feed

is live, and the wifi signal absolves
its crimes. Unplug the set, and the world
keeps watching, as eyes in silence turn
to tears. Love must never find the bend.

Jake Levine
from GHOSTING

Before you step on board, ask yourself
how much can you erase before you vanish?
What traces are you willing to lend, what secrets
do you need to conceal?
Crewing the ship one learns to feel bad
about how far you need to go
to feel bad, when you cast the net
and find yourself flapping around, gills bloodied
black eyes grayed like marble glass, caught in
this boat with shadow friends
that dissipate in ocean breeze
while sea snakes walk S shaped
off deck planks and steamed crab
blossoms white shells and brains
crack and break like cauliflower
skulls and irradiated thoughts
the gutless landscape bugs out
point their pistols up
and BANG!
cloud intestines drop
If heaven pulses like a bulging vein
the wind hurls the gulls' caws
into an El Nino squall
and the sea wails will throw you overboard
just to watch you drown
On the deck the sirens' screams
pretzel shape the fog
the fog downs the galley wall
and builds a gated community on your eyelashes

Aaaargh!
there blows a schooner
small enough for you to swallow
and *Aaargh!*
the sea dragon aches and
Aaargh!
regrets curdle like warm yogurt on the jetty rocks, but
your face already ice creams
in the lactose puddle
of your desert hot head
a mirror of batshit-iceberg-slicking life drip
crusting over the grief horizon
ripping off your eyelids
like the Bodhidharma of sleepless nights
that exhaustion won't let you fail
because among so many
you have to believe
you alone will persevere
Ghosting yourself at 3 AM
the lover's destiny is to stand in solidarity
with the monsters that want to eat them
A land lover massages their jelly fat
to become a more delicious snack
hops in the water and
the siren's glee
sounds like a colony of black ants
at the tetherball court
when the kid with a face like a dirty plate
gets pegged with a dodgeball and plops
their ice cream in the greedy sand
Despair, this ship can only be skippered by ghosts and
Departure, every hull is cramped with smacking lips
and the wanderer's heart pumps
sticky down my sweatless hand
Salvation is the wound stabbed flank

and a sea hag with seaweed hair
holding a blood tipped pen
The gunboat reports *Blast   Blast   Blast*
white flashes in the smoke filmed sky
and plop plopping
swallow corpses pound down like pepperoni shaped
nipples shaved off Zeus statues and dropped from Olympus
I read the inflated animal in the morning mirror like a bible
because the person I think I am
inside this picture of the captain
always has this feeling
I'm going to drown and
the stars spackled on the water
cackle like the glint of a pack
of smiling hyena's teeth
waiting for me at the deck end
If they break on the hull of my skull and
slosh loud in the absence of sound
My hands are like two heavy chords
an immemorial song
holding tight to the wheel

Shane Ingan
Mammon's Haiku

THIS PROPERTY IS

UNDER 24-HOUR

CAMERA SURVEILLANCE

David Harrison Horton

Model Answer (Reading)

Hear the drummer get wicked. Hell isn't for wicked drummers; it's a train station. You might argue that train stations are more like Dante's Purgatory, but that would show how little time you spend in them. Take, for example, the Wuhan station: the noodles cost 10 times, literally, what they should, the beer in the convenience shops is PBR in warm tall boys, and the design makes no sense. Was an architect even consulted? Hell is not other people, Mr. Sartre. It's poorly constructed places in which to spend time without purpose. Hear the drummer get ... Hear the drummer get ...

Model Answer (Environment)

Sometimes, just sometimes, you find a cold beer in the fridge that you forgot about. Other times, you misremember Clark Gable being in the *Missouri Breaks* with Brando. That's all wrong. You've conflated the Brando flick with *The Misfits*. What can you do? Cry in your beer? Well, you have one, unexpectedly, and it's cold. Or, you can decide to grow a mustache à la Gable. Every coin, in fact, does have two sides. That's both scientific and definitional. Look it up if you don't believe me.

Model Answer (Space Exploration)

You can envision the entirety of a skyscraper in your mind; take for example the Chrysler Building in New York. Now your brain isn't very big, but you can fit a skyscraper in it. St. Augustine said this proves you have a soul — everlasting, at that. I think it proves space is flexible. Just because black holes are fake doesn't mean we have a good grasp on the whole space-time-location situation. I mean, my girlfriend just yesterday gave me the cold shoulder.

Bobby Morris

A BIRTHDAY ALONE IN LAS VEGAS

it's my 21st
        i recognize that
people are addicted
        to rolling dings and jumping hues

slots and phones won't
        partake me and others
to drink-and-mingle

[WATCH AS MACHINES TAKE
        OVER THE TABLES]

odds don't matter,
        we base luck
off eyes' appeals

back to my room
        thought i wasn't tipsy
pop the cork off my socks
        legs like tipped-over vases

awaken from 37-minute bath,
        up and shot
blood rushed
        all is bathroom static

[HEART BEATS
        AND RIBS CAGED IT]

grip onto
      the gooseneck faucet,
hand slides the edge of a marble tub

dry focus
      into crystal water
all i see is not my reflection
      but depleted
bubbles of time

      sink back in
kill the neon,
      it's all that gets to me

Sophie Ewh

No Promises

I. **I Crocheted a Duck for You**

I have become increasingly paranoid of edits in pornography and the trucks that serve ginger lemonade at christenings. Red hair is only red in derealization nightmares. I tipped $20 on a memory and wasn't sure if I should feel good or bad. Automatons make music now but I still make things wet. There's a leaf in your thumb that won't let you speak in idioms. NASA once told me about Czech women; Did you know they sing in rounds?

II. **What happened to separating the art from the artist?**

Do you ever look at someone and see only their blue outlines. The colors Microsoft would want us to see. I asked a friend if he would ever kill himself: "No promises after 90" he said. There is a god, but they didn't put a bathroom in this club. Just oak trees and fuzzy socks. "I'm a good person" I say to the bouncer. "Yeah but did you direct Annie Hall?"

III. **Mother's Day**

I saw the stars today and they said "You need to stop creating a dialogue to fill your poems." I can't help but be afraid of French anymore. How many guitar songs must one learn before they're allowed to perform in Washington Square? Sometimes rubbing grass on your pants doesn't make you finish but it prepares an amazing casserole. Sometimes half of your friend group smokes and the other half vapes. What's your preferred form of immolation?

IV.   **Eileen is an Ex-Wife and Must Stay That Way**

Why does every Popeye's look like it was made in a studio? I locked
myself out today and thought "I am holy alone in this world." I often
think god speaks through me. I've been telling Natalie that: "If I
mistakenly say Serbia is in Russia, it's because god willed it so;" or
"god said you should lose a few if you're going to continue to put
your weight against the door." She just smiles and says "laughtrack.
loudguffaw.men&women.462837.wav."

V.   **Reasons I Love Loving**

When I'm in love, I sit backwards on my bed. I'm sitting here now. I
wear clothes that make people look at my breasts. I stop opening up
about my father and start opening up about my mother. I put coffee in
my brownies. I never choose the restaurant. I obsess over the corners of
my fingernails. I only wear deodorant after 4pm. I speak haphazardly,
like a poet on Instagram. I tell everyone how much I love them.
Everyone else. I kiss them with words, I tell them I'll write books about
them. For you, I don't write love poems; I write fan mail.

J Parker Marvin

from *A Diary of Slowly*
44234

Fracture bowl stained with water ::

the grayish residual :: the green hand
swollen and feathering in imperfect
definitions of rot :: both divergences
of time against this moment
are love ::

the smears of ink are not yet irrelevant ::
the nostalgic litter of damp paste
holds the form of words against the soft current
of a shallow wind :: there are no moments still held
in whisper ::

the sudden moan of a cow somewhere up the dark
hillside reminds the scene of place :: the
motion-sensing lights seem to click off in unison ::
there never was the expectation of witness ::
the emptiness remains :: the emptiness moves on ::

44235

The salty evaporative stain
residues are forbidden
as witnesses into the after ::
the preference is blindness ::
black blood energy ::
faint colors :: the thin passing
of faint light ::

Rectangles of capture pile up ::
we fear the impulse
of deletion :: we know we
will not look again ::
the scrolling of history
the anodyne against the
constant suddenness of birth ::
the memories of reincarnations are
reincarnations :: in the white spaces
we splice in words

Steve Gerson

Love sounds like

Love sounds
in my chest as
lightning
a tuning fork thrum

like the sky
through my fingertips
along piano keys
reverberating and

beyond thought
synapses exploding into
the quiet hum of
echoing birdsongs

Sophia Terazawa
Aptitude Test

Describe how it felt, not [desert type] [mountain type]

Describe a miracle [tablets] [range] pileup on Interstate 94

Describe [going straight to voicemail] the parking meter nested with hummingbirds

Describe whose face in a shark costume [wearing a baby shark costume underneath] grand [all day with sparklers] at the interview

Describe but don't mention a sleep study

Describe your five best [personality]

Describe in alphabetical order [skill set] [say, if the predator looks at you but doesn't attack] confidence may be called for [if, in the not-not-looking, failure might be imminent]

Describe [when the bear lunges] don't just stand there, honey

Describe success [straight-up-a-tree-gone] expect our call within four-five business days

Describe [locomotion] [debt, pod] irreparable [union] [living wage, it's not]

Describe boding [cerebrum] [thought-journey] [at the end] a blank screen

Describe how often you save your work [can you take a short survey]

Describe the bear whose forest became a torch one summer [take the survey]

Describe the gale

Describe lines running for water [skills or all you need at the end of this world]

Yesterday in my notes shells were arranged in pleasant order

Teacup and saucer filled with baby's
breath, pink roses, lily of the valley.
Wheels of fortune turned east. Iris
patchouli bundled in plastic bags.
Decay fell to one side; twice I've been
asked about a rally on Main, if I saw
my students there, if I wanted to stay
with this job, pokeweed, Prices Fork
Road, the fall semester, wintermester,
emails reminding all staff and faculty
to remain alert, but for what, I prepare
my lessons on dying. Today an
ambulance was bombed, not in this
town; syntax, nothing to throw but
ourselves. F was in my dream last
night giving birth. Who was her child
alert to disorder and order? In this
galaxy, we were all wiped out.

Sophia Terazawa

Prologue: A Call to Action

Treachery is certainly not the only path to self-determination, though one line of thought about a people's right to live and die with dignity counters annihilation.

The war machine is, and always will be, against treason. Remember that.

One line of thought is certainly not enough to stop a combat vehicle of any size. Remember who you saw in the open, in 1989, waving at the tanks to stop.

If a poem could lie down, that would be enough. If I could die for your people's right to dream, may that never be enough.

The sky records all wars as singular governance. Traitors of that state have been named among us planting soft prayers in the earth, raising their babies, calling for peace. What do I believe?

If earth records even the smallest of hopes, earth betrays no one as I betray the earth. There is no logic in naming such horror.

The war machine cannot dream. It blocks every poem, carries on down the road to every field, the same field for millennia.

At first, the poem wore a white shirt and carried, what appeared to be, nothing.

Then, the poem decided to take action.

The poem hurried out into the street.

For years, the poem remained nameless. We only saw the back of its head, the white shirt and dark trousers, how the poem gestured STOP, a period at the end of a line bringing oblivion.

Go to that period, to every line you can with that sign. The poem will fail in many ways. Still, our world is made of singing.

J. S. Graham

The tyrant's tree

The scene: a grocery store

The produce: displayed

Meat-banana abundance

Fernando Martinez Periset

"Somebody shot Ray Richards tonight"

Today's play:
"The Murder of Gonzago or The Mousetrap"
"Somebody shot Ray Richards tonight"

Yesterday… was I sitting on the roof of a crystal palace
seeing air, fire, earth and sea pouring over me?

*Between the white and yellow lights of a living city
a sixty-year-old actor rises and sails across the stage.
His rusty body bows at the audience staring at his cage,
while spotlights caress his face, old and gritty.*

*There was a time he used to enjoy
being a lonesome pretender.
But merciless winter wrecked his splendour,
crushing it down below the walls of Troy.*

Now I recall what happened that night,
when red-chested swallows talked to the shimmering tune of moonlight
asking her to whiten their feathers;
when the sweet morning dew slipped away from the tip of my tongue
and came through the ceiling of this golden hall.
An iron jungle, a concrete cage
where undone shadows wander in ecliptic obscurity…
I could have made my body roam
through the empty streets of a sunless sky
that bathed the marshmallow houses.
I wish I could have drowned in the lagoon
where glass mermaids sang day, night and noon.

They say I have always been ill, very ill.

Standing ovation in some forsaken place,
beside the West End lights,
praising Ray Richard's suit
whose right sleeve laughs, whose left sleeve cries.

In the distance I saw a yellow land
where the building walls turn to paper flames
and the clouds were made of clay.
The edifices crumbling, falling above the moon.
This plastic floor moving faster
than a sinking ship on the edge of a stormy waterfall.

The rustling echoes of dead voices told me! It was not my fault!
They whispered in my ear… They told me to do it.
And a million shady eyes trapped in a crystal cage.
I took my pen out, turned over the page,
looking for the man standing on the stage. [Heartbeat.]
An ink-stream that will forever rest in this verse. [Heartbeats.]
His dead heart shrieked; still stayed mine, though I was alive.

Ray Richards collapses with a red stain in his chest
on his white, fragile suit
as the tide rises to this verse's pace,
over the fragments of Ray Richards.

I wake up in the morning in this palace made of glass.
No darkness. No light. No stars.

The police said: "We know it was you, though he was in your head."
"But that's silly!" I said. "You cannot kill whom does not exist, can you?
Such a poor poet I am! How could I have done such thing?"
[The beating of his hideous heart]

When I touch my nakedness, I feel the itch of red ink
on my white, fragile suit.
And lose sense of time and space
when my own pen stabs my chest.
My right sleeve laughs, my left sleeve cries.
Standing an hour upon the stage,
half alive and half enduring a disease called age,
I witness myself in the mirror aiming at my own reflection.
[Your sighs. My gaze. His life. Your face. My eyes]

And they said I had always been ill, very ill.

Jennifer Weigel
Grief

I sit

                                        alone

                    adrift

Time passes.

....
....
....
....
....
....
....
....
....
....
....
....
....
....
....
....
....
....
....
....

I wait.

My

breath

is

still

slow.

My

heart

is

still

heavy.

The

ache

is

still

there.

The

silence

is^1

---

1 ... *

Jennifer Weigel

footnotes to the footnote

*agonizing
*aimless
*alarming
*alien
*aloof
*anguished
*anxious
*apathetic
*apparent
*arduous
*awkward
*bleak
*caustic
*cheerless
*cold
*comfortable
*complex
*confounding
*confusing
*consuming
*corroding
*damaging
*deafening
*debilitating
*degenerative
*depressing
*despairing
*destructive
*detrimental
*directionless
*disconcerting
*disengaging

*disheartening
*dismal
*disorienting
*disquieting
*distant
*distressing
*dreadful
*dreary
*empty
*encompassing
*endless
*enduring
*eternal
*everything
*exacerbating
*excruciating
*foreign
*forlorn
*ghastly
*gloomy
*great
*grievous
*harmful
*harrowing
*heavy
*holy
*immeasurable
*immediate
*immense
*impairing
*inaccessible
*incoherent
*inconsolable
*indifferent
*indistinct

*infinite
*inherent
*insignificant
*invisible
*isolating
*joyless
*laborious
*lasting
*limitless
*lingering
*long
*maddening
*massive
*melancholic
*miserable
*mistaken
*misunderstood
*monumental
*mortifying
*morose
*mournful
*nauseating
*noxious
*numbing
*obscure
*omnipresent
*oppressive
*otherworldly
*painful
*paramount
*pervasive
*present
*regretful
*relatable
*remorseful

*reticent
*saddening
*somber
*sorrowful
*superficial
*tedious
*terrifying
*tormenting
*torturous
*trivial
*troublesome
*trying
*ubiquitous
*unapproachable
*unattainable
*unclear
*uncomfortable
*unpleasant
*unrelenting
*unsettling
*unworldly
*upsetting
*urgent
*vast
*vexing
*visceral
*woeful
*worsening
*wretched
*... the rest is silence

DIS.ORIENTATIONS

BEE LB
Spencer Jayu Ward
Dinçer Güçyeter   Caroline Wilcox Reul
Richie Magnia
Esenia Banuelos
Yonatan Berg   Joanna Chen
Glen Armstrong
Edward Burke
Kenton K. Yee
Wei Shao
Thom Eichelberger-Young
J. Catcher Ward
M. Vasalis   Arno Bohlmeijer
N.T. Chambers
Maria da Cunha   Bernardo Villela
Kris Falcon
Kevin LeMaster

Wetland March

The only wilderness I've known is tall grass, swishing
against unshaven legs, bugs twitching their way
through the blades, away from the body's intrusion.
I've seen a cicada uncase itself, startled by the desperate
electric shame they emit. I am lost to myself aside from my
bent body's reflection rippling over water, trying to make sense
of what is seen. I am lost to myself aside from standing in bulrush,
eyes closed, wishing on endless seeds for a recognizable self. I am lost
to myself aside from looking up in the midst of trees towering taller
than I thought possible, my own body so inescapably scant.
But the awe wears off, given enough time. A nine hour trek
makes everything new. Makes the world smaller than before
you traversed it. My legs refuse to carry me far, lock tight, send signals
I've learned to ignore. My body follows my will in pursuit of other's
pride. My body's punishment follows suit. My spine relents
under the weight of my failing body, curves low, trembles.
The rush of wind from a great height feels like a far off whisper.
A memory left so long I wonder if it was only a dream.
I've known a loose foothold better than a tight grasp.
Questioned ivy & ticks & mosquitoes & leeches.
The only wilderness I've known is rushing water, open-faced
rockside blurring in my peripheral. Steep drops
above & below. The sky indescribable
as anything but wide open. Stars so bright I dream
of catching them. Reaching up & making them mine.
The awe wears off given enough time. I have too much
& not enough of it, same as the rest of you.

Spencer Jayu Ward
In Transit >>> ICN, SEOUL

My love always seems held less as a living choice, homeward bound,
than an object in transit, still momentarily detained
by women concerned far more with questioning doldrums,
partitioning bona fides, than admitting any answers

<<<<<<<<<<<<<<<<<<<<<<<<<<<<<<<<<<<< *Where is it coming from?*
"In Korea, it is very seldom that people travel beyond their own area." >>>>>
<<<<<<<<<<<<<<<<<<<<<<<<<<<<<<<<<<<<< *What is its destination?*
"I stepped off the plane and onto U.S. soil for the first time in my life." >>>>>
<<<<<<<<<<<<<<<<<<<<<<<<<<<<<<<<<<<<<<< *When was it born?*
"7:15 AM, February 15, 1972" >>>>>>>>>>>>>>>>>>>>>>>>>>>>>>>>>>>>>>>
<<<<<<<<<<<<<<<<<<<<<<<<<<<<<<<<<<< *Can it prove its place of origin?*
"From hearing the missionaries' stories, I had been very excited about coming here.">
<<<<<<<<<<<<<<<<<<<<<<< *Any foreign or hazardous articles to be declared?*
"My feelings changed when I saw so many colors of hair and skin with my own
eyes; I was scared.">>
<<<<<<<<<<<<<<<<<<<<<<<<<< *Is the purpose of its visit business, or pleasure?*
"I didn't know how to communicate with them; we were afraid of each other.">
<<<<<<<<<<<<<<<<<<<<<<<<<<<<<<<< *How long does it intend on staying?*
"Now I have made all kinds of friends, and it seems like having magic." >>>>>>
<<<<<<<<<<<<<<<<<<<<<<<<<<<<<<<<<< *What is its point of departure?*
"I have found a person can come from outside this country and become part of it.">

For my love to simply persist, never seems to warrant much
more than a temporary issuance of blanket entry
into, what has continually proven itself to be,
the less than prevailing state of affairs, dearly departed

Dinçer Güçyeter
die grüne Strickjacke

in diesem Garten haben Schmetterlinge an einem Februarabend /
nachdem das schlafende weiße Fohlen unter Flocken aufgefunden wurde
/ zu Saz getanzt / auf dem Diwan der Derwische lag der offene Sarg / in
diesem Garten / auf ihm das grüne Tuch / geschleudert von Gebeten einer
Frau / die dieser Welt kein Wort mehr zu sagen hatte / das letzte, was ich
von ihr hörte *weder eine Beerdigung noch eine Hochzeitsfeier darf in diesem
Leben verschoben werden* / das ist die größte Sünde / ich war damals so alt
wie die Schaukel unter der Dachrinne

wisst ihr, wie majestätisch eine Handschrift sein kann? / in diesem Garten
/ am Eingang / hängt noch der vergilbte Brief zwischen Tür und Rahmen
Liebster Papa,
ich bin jetzt seit 2 Monaten in Deutschland, mir geht's gut, die
Tarhana-Suppe und der frische Käse fehlen mir ein wenig. habe jetzt einen
Arbeitsplatz in der Fabrik, werde gut verdienen und wer weiß, vielleicht kann ich
mir sogar bald einen Mercedes kaufen. ich lege einen 100-Mark-Schein mit in den
Umschlag. kannst du bitte, wenn du wieder in die Stadt fährst, mit diesem Geld für
Mutter 5 Meter Seide kaufen. sie soll sich ein neues Kleid schneidern lassen und
stolz damit durch das Dorf laufen, stolz wie ein Pfau. noch lebe ich in einer
Arbeiter-WG, wenn ich meine eigene Wohnung habe, schicke ich euch die Papiere
vom Amt, damit könnt ihr ein Visum beantragen. in stiller Sehnsucht umarme ich
euch beide.
Yilmaz / Köln, 1966
wisst ihr / manchmal sind die Jahre schneller auf der Reise als die
Briefe

in diesem Garten / auf dem nackten Zweig des Magnolienbaums webt
ein Ameiseknäuel Abschiede aus Seidenfäden / und diese Krähen / die
verstummt auf dem Fahrrad sitzen / wisst ihr / wie viele Sprachen sie

translated from German by Caroline Wilcox Reul
The Green Cardigan

in this garden on a February evening / after the sleeping white colt
was discovered buried under flakes / butterflies danced to the bağlama
/ in this garden / the coffin lay open on the divan of the dervishes /
across it the green cloth / flung from the prayers of a woman / who had
nothing more to say to this world / the final word I heard from her,
neither a funeral nor a wedding should ever be put off in this life / that is
the greatest sin / at the time I was the same age as the swing under the
drainpipe

do you know how majestic the written hand can be? / in this garden /
at its entrance / the yellowed letter still hovers between door and frame
Dearest Papa,
I've been in Germany for two months now, I'm doing well, though
sometimes I long for tarhana soup and fresh cheese. I found work
in a factory, will earn good money and who knows, maybe I
can buy myself a Mercedes someday. I'm enclosing 100 marks in
the envelope. When you go into town again, could you buy mother five
meters of silk with it. She should have a dress made and wear
it though the village, proud as a peacock. I still live with others
from the factory, when I get my own place, I'll send you the immigration
paperwork so you can apply for a visa. In quiet yearning I embrace
you both,
Yilmaz, Cologne, 1966
do you know / sometimes the years undertake their journey faster than
the mail

in this garden / on the bare branches of the magnolia a skein of ants
weaves each departure from silken thread / and the silenced crows /
perched on the bicycle / do you know / how many languages they speak

verstehen / diese Stille wiegt mehr als alle Sprachen der Welt / und frage jetzt nicht / ob eine Sprache was wiegen kann / ich sah / wie eine Silbe zu einer Walze wurde, wie sie diese Erde zu Leinen formte / vergiss nicht / hinter jedem Leinen kühlt sich eine verbrannte Zunge

in diesem Garten spielt jetzt ein kleiner Junge mit seinem Ball / in dem Riss seiner Hose ist ein Pult angeheftet / dort legt der DJ Ronaldo die Platten von Prince auf / gestern wurde der Junge von seinem Trainer in eine andere Mannschaft geschickt / er muss noch lernen, sich an die Regeln zu halten / später darf er vielleicht wieder zurück / der Junge schießt den Ball über den Zaun und schreit Tooooooor / am Abend im Bett sagt er mir:
Papa, wer weiß, vielleicht bin ich eines Tages ein Profi–Fußballer / werde vielleicht soooooo reich sein und kann mir ein Cabrio kaufen, damit fahre ich dich dann zu Aldi, versprochen! und lach nicht, Papa, du weißt, in meine neue Mannschaft kommen nur die Besten
ich hoffe, Schatz, die Jahre sind nicht schneller als die Träume / und jetzt / mach die Äugelchen zu und schlafe / wir haben morgen was Großes vor / ich werde dir den See-Drachen zeigen

und da, hinter dem Fenster sitzt ein Mann am Schreibtisch, zerstümmelt die Worte mit Erinnerungen / schaut aus dem Fenster / sieht im Garten den Diwan der jungen Knaben / auf ihren Nabeln die Kupfergewichte der Sprache / auf einem verrosteten Käfig unter Flocken sieht er die grüne Strickjacke / und denkt / wie viele unsichtbare Knoten dieses Gedicht doch hat

/ this silence weighs more than all languages in the world / and don't you ask / whether a language can weigh anything / I saw / how a syllable became a roller, how it shaped the earth to linen / don't forget / behind every linen cloth a burned tongue cools

in this garden a little boy plays with his ball / a stage hangs at a tear in his jeans / where DJ Ronaldo spins records by Prince / yesterday the boy was sent to another team by his coach / he needs to learn to follow the rules / they might let him back later / the boy shoots the ball over the fence and bellows goooooal / that evening at bedtime he says to me:
Papa, who knows, maybe someday I'll be a pro footballer / I might get sooooo rich, I can buy me a convertible, then I'll drive you to Costco, promise! and don't laugh, Papa, you know, only the best players are allowed on my team
I hope, son, the years don't pass faster than your dreams / and now / close your sleepy eyes and drift off / we have a big day tomorrow / I will show you the dragon of the lake

and there behind that window, a man sits at his desk, maims words with his memories / gazes out the window / sees in the garden the divan of the boys / on their navels the copper weights of language / on a rusted cage under snowflakes he sees the green cardigan / and thinks / how many invisible knots this poem must have

Richie Magnia

An Artist's Submission

"Color is my day-long obsession, joy and torment." -Claude Monet

You're fascinating and intoxicating and I just might let you kill me.
Dig your fingers into my eyes until all I see is you and my own blood.
It's perfectly normal to only see you and my own blood.
Denial.

It wasn't until I met you that I acknowledged the boil in my stomach,
the parasite boroughing beneath my skin, but what is it looking for?
It must be you; your selfish need to make yourself a home. After all—
You're fascinating and intoxicating, but I won't let you kill me.

Please don't leave. I don't care if you'll kill me. I'll give you that boy.
The boy in my bones whose hands are not yet dirty. Suck on his bones.
    Devour him whole.
God was once a boy, but he was devoured by Man. You can devour me
    the same.
Denial, Anger, Bargaining.

I'm at the point where I don't know if I am real or not, but I know you are.
I am the Forgotten Man of 1934 and I don't know my own name.
My body is weak and bleeding, left hollow by you. Will I ever be filled
    again?
You're fascinating and intoxicating and I'm begging you to kill me.

I've asked myself if you are worth it, even if no one knows my name.
Months and years have passed and I think it is. Because of you.
To be an artist is to submit to Obsession on bleeding kneecaps.
Denial, Anger, Bargaining, Depression, Acceptance.

What silly words — silly words of how I have thought of you every moment, words that turn into words that turn into creation that turn into you. You're fascinating and intoxicating and you're going to kill me.
Denial, Anger, Bargaining, Depression, Acceptance. Submission.

Esenia Banuelos

A Portrait of My Father and Grandfather Laboring in Southern California (In The Shape of Leaves)

Remnants of your reanimation are strewn about every sidewalk; bleeding instances of your billowy intestines as autumnal tears and crushed twigs under leather. I have accumulated you with my eyes; you are a portrait of memory, skin, and blood in shades of decay. How pieces of you ripped from the joint and flew out towards dirt-heavens and concrete-hells, and how your conquered conglomerate bled out from under car-bodies. You are a red-fine for the season until you are too carmine to complement pristine shaved-ecosystems; you are brown, and only good in moderation. You're as common as mud under their heels; you're always a newfound gold between my fingers. I watch your body be reassembled in little exhibits across campus; inoffensive and charitable in your spatial existence. I take from your body and splay you across every patio, Princeton roof, and every porch, where you become the seasonal reminder of laborious love. One day, it will come that I will leave you as you were gathered, and by then, I will be but an additional nuisance to rake; my bones, an unaesthetic breakage of your blood.

limpieza///

en los montes no se aprende leer / se
aprende cantar / y haci poesías atrapaban
vírgenes / la manda español filtra por la
ventana / arrastrando fetos / mama
pensaba que con leer / semen de leche 'te
amo' / hímenes desvanecen en sal /
mujermorena dique la palabra era fórmula
/ eye render infer / tile / eye lurn woman
fone / tikly / mama sung tú mi en la cuna
to kip mi barren / dijo que no me dejaba /
quedar blanca como su vientre / y cuando
dejo mis cobijas y mandilas hechas leches
/ que protegen / del ojo malo y baboso /
no me lavaria con yemas ni salvia / eye
opun da book of skin / may be eye caym
tú hav mi seel / pulvur eyes /

yu don lurn tú reed en da montyns / yu
lurn to syng / and thats howe poems cot
virgins / da spanish order filturs fru the
windowe / trawling fetuses / mama thot
that tú reed / milksemen "i luv yew" /
hymen dizolv en salt / brownwoman say
that wird es formula / eye render infer /
tile / ay lurn woman fone / tikly / mama
sung tú mi en the crib to kip mi barren /
tells mi not tú let miself / bi wite like hir
wum / and wen eye leav mi linens and
vayls of milk / that protek mi / from evil
and lussful eyes / eye won wash myself
with yolk nor salvia / eye opun da book
of skin / may be eye caym tú hav mi seel /
pulvur eyes

Yonatan Berg

בלבול

בָּלוֹן תּוֹעֶה מֵאִיר עֶרֶב שֶׁעוֹמֵד
בְּגוֹן מַהֲדוּרַת הַחֲדָשׁוֹת.
הַיֶּלֶד בּוֹכֶה אֲבָל עֵינֵי צוֹחֲקוֹת
הַמַּגִּישָׁה יָפָה וּשְׁמוֹת מֵתִים עוֹלִים מִגְּרוֹנָהּ.
עַכְשָׁו עָלַי לְהַשְׁמִיעַ מוּזִיקָה הַמַּתְאִימָה
לְרִקּוּד, דַּוְקָא כִּי אֲנִי עִם עַצְמִי
וְלֹא נִשְׁאַר בִּי כֹּחַ כְּלָל.
עָלֵינוּ לִצְעֹק רָטֹב כְּשֶׁבַּחוּץ אוֹגוּסְט,
לִלְחֹשׁ עַכְשָׁו, בְּדִיּוּק כָּכָה, זֶה נָעִים,
לְסָדִין מְקֻמָּט וְרֵיק.
הַדִּיסְלֶקְצְיָה הַיָּפָה שֶׁל הַלֵּב
מַעֲבִירָה אוֹתִי בָּעוֹלָם,

מְבֻלְבָּל וּמְפֻזָּר כְּמוֹ אוֹהֲבִים בַּלַּיְלָה הָרִאשׁוֹן.

translated from Hebrew by Joanna Chen
Confusion

An errant balloon interrupts an evening
consumed by the latest news bulletin,
a boy weeps on the street but my eyes fill
with color, the anchorwoman is beautiful,
the names of the dead rising up
in her throat.

Now I'm here by myself
and I have no strength left, none at all.
Now I must shout *first rain!* when outside it's October,
now I must whisper *good night!* to a crumpled sheet
on an empty bed.

I confuse the dream with the awakening
the sea with the desert, the coming
with going. I paint the window ledge with sugar
I shatter glass under a canopy of white.
The heart's beautiful dyslexia
leads me through the world

Confused and shattered like lovers on their first night.

ימי תפילה

אֶת הַצְּעָקָה אֲנַחְנוּ לוֹקְחִים מֵהָאַיִל
וְאֶת הַכְּנִיעָה מִצֶּבַע הַטַּלִּיתוֹת.
נְגּוּנִים הֵם פָּנָסִים קְטַנִּים בַּמְּנָהָרָה חֲשׁוּכָה,
אַתֶּם רָצִים וּמִשְׁתּוֹלְלִים כְּפִי שֶׁהָיִיתִי
רוֹצֶה לְהִתְפַּלֵּל. אַל תִּלְמְדוּ מֵהַמִּלִּים
פֹּה, הָאֵל אֵינוֹ מַעֲבִיר וּמוֹנֶה,
הוּא הַגַּעְגּוּעַ וְהַבְּרִיזָה.

הַתְּשׁוּבָה וְהַתְּפִלָּה וְהַצְּדָקָה שֶׁלִּי הַשָּׁנָה
הֵן לָקַחַת אֶתְכֶם לְמָחֳרָת לַמַּעְיָן
כְּדֵי שֶׁתּוּכְלוּ לְהַגִּיד בְּעוֹד שָׁנִים,
אָז, בְּרֹאשׁ הַשָּׁנָה, בַּמַּיִם הַקָּרִים, הִתְחַבַּקְנוּ.

Days of Prayer

We take roar from a ram
We take submission from a tallis.
Melodies are flashlights in a tunnel.
You run and rage the way I want to pray.
Do not learn from these words,
God is neither conduit nor counter
God is yearning and breeze.
Atonement and prayer and charity this year
Is to take you to a spring in the Judean Hills
So you will be able to say in years to come
Back then, in cold water, we embraced.
Under a fig tree I realize I have leaned on poetry
For too long. It is the word that contains us,
an old prayer of mine, suddenly embodied.

Glen Armstrong
Antonyms for "Beyond"

There are no sensibilities,
only touching,

only noises that wrench
me from my self

as if from sleep.
Identity slumbers until

strangers collide
in the street.

•

I have been interested
in fingers and toes

since I was a baby.
It's as if I have been training

for this moment all my life.

Edward Burke

Calibrations of Khlebnikov

Khlebnikov on empty pointless field of carbon night:
empty field ignites the text, the One the Only Book,
pointless field accommodates the poet's burning text.
(Terminal velocity poet, field, and text attain.)

Khlebnikov when stepping out was sometimes struck by birds.
Once, when sculpting air outside, he struck some moving birds.

Khlebnikov upon a time found one dimension lost:
      in radial volume sank he down, without and with no height,
      to excavated floors of black labyrinth he droppt.
Some other time, Khlebnikov is spun 'round in an arc,
      a spiral of height or a spiral of depth,
      to find himself possessed of spiral voice.
Yet always at all times his hidden space:
      Khlebnikov so cloaked in time his lice forget to squirm,
      Caucasian trains and Caspian ships refuse to let them board.

The cayenne calendars, paprika clocks of capitals
were never synchronized with the archaic King of Time—
the defects of their months, their minutes lost and soon forgot,
abandoned in a blank abyss from which no days returned,
their crusts and crumbs dispersed and disappeared—
Khlebnikov saw nothing to retrieve or memorize:
the pages Khlebnikov has amply read and justly torn
      become blue butterflies to all imperiled minotaurs.

—as from the Second Sea of blue do frozen arrows fall,
up through the selfsame Sea of blue our poisoned arrows fly:

and undeterred does Khlebnikov stretch out, still resolute—
"Man seems on his own carbon choked to death"—
white storks and mountain sparrows, banded warblers, all agree:
from his remote and rustic roost, the King of Time has ruled,
kind Velimir the First enunciating his decrees.

A Quotidian Mystery

Some die from butter on baked potatoes

My survival's a cellular lineup
tangled like cat-played yarn

mother's blameless sins vitiated her capacities
father's gut guilty as a politician's

peripheral aunts and ancestors never met
would barely rescind my surmises

My 91st wasn't a party it wasn't
a dirge
no one invited
nobody came
some were thinking of me
I thought

a January cloudburst delivered like an overture
let me know there's a leak in my roof

Though it rained all day
I contained a strange happiness, never disclaiming
the pills I count coldly
while I take in the sunsets Capricorns get
in winter

my sense of wonder

and when it's not about beauty
I think about hands

catching CNN at day's end
a woman's prayerful hands
in Kyiv begging a journalist
For what, for what?

Kenton K. Yee

Wormholes

I was underwater, weightless, inside a cave with bubbles rising and disappearing into the sky. I had fins, a mouth—gills, and hips stiff as wood. The cave walls were clear as water but hard as rock. On my side: ferns, gravel, an elephant with curly tusks, and sounds—sounds I know now to be footsteps, voices. Laughter. Food snowed in from the sky. I slept and ate more and more. The last things I saw: a monster behind the wall and a giraffe licking the elephant's back as a giant cobweb came down and lifted me into blinding light.

> walking the dog
> I let each fire hydrant
> tell me a dream

Department of the Interior

suits and dresses
I hang out with
the linen

Desire isn't key. Sense is. We sense, make sense, and
therefore we survive.

Warm eggs
in a tree
white omelet

It makes sense to be sensible. The way your heart beats
faster in the presence of beauty is dangerous.

thrush and sequoias
on the subway
everyone's a sardine

Wei Shao
Linguistic Disability

... to Brooklyn…Indian English Korean English British English American English Chinese Irish English Jewish English Englishes English just English just Paper…

English can be a song in Chinese

Chinese in English is Chinglish

Which language is better?

In the spatial constellation, who are we?

monolingual' bilingual' trilingual' quadrilingual' pentalingual, which-lingual

Who is more important, you or your language?
How to understand each other with so many languages?

Indian English Korean English British English American English Irish English Jewish English
Englishes Englishes Yours Ours His Hers Mine Theirs Its

Where are we in language?

In the bad luck month of Lily's Valley

MY ENGLISH MY CHINESE MY ENGLISHES MY CHINESES

Just a sunflower bitch

And, you are disabled

Story of Dragon

Every hometown has a story of the dragon

Young people should go out to try the world. Like the ducks

In folklore, they swam into an upstream rock hole and showed up

Downstream years later. If they had never left, there would be no story;

If they left and never showed up, their story would be tragic; if they left

and came back, their story would become glorious.

If ducks could end up somewhere else,

Could you do the same?

You could end up

Being somewhere else and becoming new.

Thom Eichelberger-Young
Love Story #9

I

When you met me I was still counting windows
in all the boys' houses one two three four.
Only to explain a way in which I am autistic.

Tapestry. I think you said
you *left me behind in the hot air balloons,*
cords dangling, latent gossamer pilling
on my new sweater. You said *it is too busy.*

Last night, wishing I knew more
about chemistry. Gazing at a shoebox,
you are breathing. Watching the movie,
you realize we are all going to die. You miss
the cherry from the cordial.

Never a hand to say I'm sorry. A door
you could have opened any time, so many
times we rode in your car. Spend it with my firstborn,
you know you need just rethink it and realize
she has her reasons. She flew United.

Just in time, bottle opened or she is
having eye surgery. C—remembers he needs
glasses. Everybody's having it done, even
the poor ones. Says nothing. *Have you traveled?*

We used to live inside the arm. Held aloft,
it was warmer when he was sweaty. Representing

each moon in orbit, the popcorn pieces
only surrender emotion to a rational solution.

Why all the money? It's just a sweater.
Not knowing the measurements, and each other
precision takes too long to imagine. Done by hand,
or should we say, by eye. No machines to diminish
this process to automation and affordability.

Consider what it means to be in reach.
Too long spent saying *I love you*
while touching any and every difference.

His weight the presence no need to label
what came before and after
you already knew, wondering if it wasn't, too,
any good thing about a glacier melting.

More and more, you realize you need
a life without the internet and battle machines
presenting their influential livery for everyone to see
money's inhibitions forget nowhere and nobody.

A story about what you loved,
a story I want so much to tell you. But, too late,
learned too late and leaving only my stomach
to churn with regret for hate and misplaced love.

Day edging into evening passes, Midwestern shades
and all weather visible from your balcony. Abandoned
city light flashes automatically for several months untended.
In darkness, broken glass below becomes glowworms,
uneasy shards glinting mirrors all the wrong shades
of metallic yellow before the moonlight. Thoraxes
purple at dusk and jet at midnight, all while the light
goes on flashing, me or him smoking and watching
the bugs flight, remaining eerily unmoving.

My eyes saw what my hands did in the car
humming lines the kids'll never know.
References running through my head the way she
collides over the slits of white paint. Gleeful
-ly ignorant, she glides state through state
without compensation in tow for her victims.
All unknowing, their driving, just wanting sushi
at discount on Wednesday from the local grocer.

Although, each store was a chain of some or other
franchise, family conglomerate, feeder into body
of a corporation. There are rumors they war, some
supermarket mafia. We imagine the bodies, stacked
between Progresso soup cans and aluminum pie tins.
Through many nights, they lie rotting. Reminders
of the avarice of their aisles.

Millions of conversations permeate themselves viruses
across the Amtrak map on the executive's wall.
All places touched by your voice, even as eerie to think
years after we last spoke and to never speak again,
dialogue continues. *Dialogue*, I mutter, pages loose
and living aside. *So much for that*, stricken by memories
of my aversion to prose and it's need for more

than my simplicity. Voice box, I held a workshop once
intricate in nature and failing to accomplish much.
Nothing but words to the wall, and indeed in time I did
do this and that to pin bits of scrap and stamp post-its
across the spaces above my desks, thinking it would aid
in the geometry I believed was structure. *C—*

Silence murmurs as wind, unsettling the way it cuts
my jackets off and leaves me still cold. I thought I was more
prepared than this, I thought I had gloves. Somethings,
you know, are better left forgotten. Our electric game
we play in your living room by the new sofa. Woeful,
bird lowing in the night, disorienting sounds mixing
with esophagitis and the knowledge the nearest cow
sleeps fifteen miles south. Game escalates, becomes drama
off-Broadway. Nylon sting. Wondering when the cops
will be called. Foggy, I stumble away and exit through
the stage door, into my car, and drive away.

Although, in the dream I don't return, in reality, nearing
midnight, the light still pulses. At times furiously, hopeful
as death throes to extinguish, but then churning into slowness
again, our neighborhood misery restored. Much like that yelling,
or the echoes in back woods behind the house, in childhood.
This time, it's your mother screaming something to do with socks,
left on the stairs or abandoned before washing. What stands
out into the noise of nothing is the cockatoo, callously spitting
her words into the back yard for all the other houses to hear
into their soup, whispering rumors and telling stories over
through the next day. Diurnal mystery of the neighborhood.

J. Catcher Ward

The Shadow Body

Sit in the
faint light and
let me tell you about the shadow
body.
A stillness, a whirling disk.
How do I peel back the silence
of limbs
and reach the place of the faces?
It starts where the body isn't
And there are many.
Somewhere else
beyond the reach of
one

M. Vasalis

Felix was blank
met bruine haren en een zachte g.

En: hij was kleurenblind, hij keek met scheef
getild gezicht en toegeknepen ogen naar de lucht.
Ik deed het heimelijk na. Wat heb ik hem bemind
toen ik vijf jaar was. Hij was negen.
Er is een bruine foto van ons allen aan de waterkant
gezeten in het gras, en daarop houd ik vlak
boven zijn hoofd, zijn verend haar mijn hand,
kijk met ZIJN toegeknepen ogen (onherroepelijk kleurenblind)
omhoog, je ziet de ouders en de kinderen en de zomerwind
die het gras scheef waait en in al die haren woelt –
je ziet dat ogenblik dat toentertijd nog eeuwig was.

M. Vasalis
uit: 'De oude kunstlijn', 2002

translated from Dutch by Arno Bohlmeijer

Felix was white
with brown hair and a light dialect

And: he was color-blind, his face looked lop-
sided and his eye squinted at the sky.
I copied that secretly. How dearly I loved him
at the age of five. He was nine.
There's a brown picture of us all by the waterside,
sitting in the grass, where I have my hand right
above his head, his bouncing hair, and
looking up with *his* squinting eyes (definitely color-blind),
seeing the parents and the children and the summer wind
that blows the grass aslant and fumbles in so much hair –
the instant shows that eyeblink, still eternal at the time.

N.T. Chambers
Mistaken Identity

Sometimes, when
the three
hundred or
so miles
of this
mandatory exile
add up to more than
all the icy-planted
rails that tie me
to my
out-of-context self,
memories of hot dog
afternoons with
dazzling sunsets
bring back
nearly
forgotten
emotions that found
some relief
in a suntanned
August evening spirit,
who didn't quite know
where to begin with me
or how to read
the crossroads look.

Summer came late last year
it was all right -
if anything,

a bit too concerned
with walking on ahead
then looking back
to a someone
who was never
really there.

Maria da Cunha

O nevoeiro cresceu envolvendo a cidade

O nevoeiro cresceu envolvendo a cidade
Num manto pardacento: Eu continuo só:
Meus olhos cuidam ver, a baça claridade,
um monge carmelita a resurgir do pó.

Outro...mais outro ainda...animam-se as ruínas
Em profundo silencio, através das ogivas,
Eles passam talvez para rezar matinas
Co'a sombra do capuz nas faces pensativas.

Lá vai, humilde frade, o grande Condestável!
Não mais há de brandir a espada formidável!
Nos combates, não mais ele há de erguer a voz!

Sombras que deslisais numa brancura d'astro,
Não podeis entender-me, ó vultos de alabastro:
Cinco séculos vão passados sobre vos!

translated from Portuguese by Bernardo Villela

The fog grew enveloping the city

The fog grew enveloping the city
in a silvery mantle: I continue alone:
My eyes look carefully, the steamy clarity,
A Carmelite monk resurgent from the dust.

Another   but another entirely   animated the ruins
in profound silence, through ogival arches,
They took, perhaps, to praying matins,
With hood-shade on pensive faces.

There goes, humble friar, the great Captain!
No more will you brandish a formidable sword!
In battles, no more will he raise his voice!

Shadows that slide in a star's whiteness,
cannot understand me, the alabaster figures;
five centuries go passing over you!

Kris Falcon

Part-Timer Mid-Orbit

Skipper of a cracked step. But hide-and-seek
overstayer. Second-guesser yet compulsive
über-archer. In the park, underreaching.
Down-scoring at the arcade.
Wherever I flew. On the tiles of a motel,

tried to piece back a monument to see if it would
mist riverside again. The real mouth dried up.
Find me a hazard I'll turn a pond.
Early on, I made the cut into a kitchen for saying
assisting would not feel complete until I educated.

In between I gleaned part- some full-
time with scraps to pass. Happy orbit!
indeed. In between I unstitched my coat, moved
to town where I'd run into my ex, who side-eyed me
like I came to collect. Jack of all spades.

Dropout? Caver? Not tags I pin. I can only
gold-dig my pocket. Given exact, queued.
Known intros by heart. I haven't asked
to switch seats. I own no shades.
Let a line crease my face. My garland grows

angular. I thought of toil as many motherless under
noon sun, looking up to heavens the pyramid
will lead their queen to. Terms look like rain.
But my father: Stop thinking of law as abstract.
Later, my father: Start with integrity.

One job lasted a year plus. I thought level up.
None of that this too shall pass as I waded, interludeist
in a pool past three, Wednesday of a summit
before both earlobes were in. And my arms
made a ripple, like it could cast a frequency.

Carayan

The word for river, I gather also for the rest
of the deep waters toward high seas—
a novel flowing to poem. *K* up north,

where once upon a time fishermen had no need
to farm mullets more prized than mother-
of-pearl. Purple sky stormed;

the tide delivered president's fish.
Boatloads before a net was cast.

As with lobsters shown on *Bizarre Foods*
in New England in America
centuries ago. These days

an angler can trawl all night
farther out from the bay, from dusk in rain,
homegrown RnB. Those dreams of gold stalks,

credit full, juice from husks, just to bring home
a Styrofoam of silverfish-family. Lord willing.

If it is brought back then it was owed—
sounds sound in the market.

Those who recall the champion chuckle on
the flavor's smell—shades of fried mackerel scad
and skate, monsooned-on lagoons.

Clear seabed. Fisherfolk can bellow and plead
all they want at waves, the break
that knows best these rhythms only form

U of a circle. But never once debtor,
mother nature.

Lore of islands. No handful heed
the howl of ghosts who traded their last glimmer
mid-sea, from the start.

Who can't keep the foot in the door
from sinking? Debate this

season sees barge after barge cross
rims. Foresees huts slam stilt by stilt

on soft earth. Who has been? Where is
whose shame in a string of humid siestas

condensing spills, drifts. Till brine, spit, thin air.
Always in the ether, in the rationed
metro I'm asked a new @. Feels more South

than West bait. Sometimes the ancient name
for stream, the root too

of the province where Ma was born, black-
pearls. Unlocks a security question.

Kevin LeMaster

Before Your Heart

       stopped abruptly beating
and the wooden signs, placed

like warnings, each word,
signifying your date of

death, we felt the wind
of your name, burn into our backs.

your car, cradle empty,
left running with door wide

open like a mouth,
consuming you whole.

you existed in a world
that didn't want to know

you, who would have rather
forgotten you than to acknowledge

your existence. your children
miss your ghosted texts,

your puff of smoke disappearing
act, and so we remember you

by the faded picture collage at the
edge of town, staked like permanence

and wonder where you've gone,
where you've been all these years.

DISILLUSION;
DISSOLUTION

Rowan Tate

Park Joon   Susan Kim

Will Neuenfeldt

Mia Lindenburg

Whitney Schmidt

Lawrence Bridges

Karoline von Günderrode   Alani Rosa Hicks-Bartlett

Chen Poyu   Nicholas Wong

Guy D'Annolfo

Lina Odeh

Akhmet Baitursynuly   Jake Zawlacki

B.A. Van Sise   Eleanora Foglia

A. J. Bermudez

Eugene Datta

Helen Steenhuis

David Romanda

Rowan Tate

postcard from home

the world we were in is overgrown
with the pit-pierced places in us we were afraid to give a name
and sharper lines of sight.
in it, we go foraging for selves
across the sword-swish of time in the fall of its folds,
unpeeling pasts from presents, the moth of a memory
skewered
with a toothpick to the
yolk-yellow lamplight of this childhood bedroom
where i am five years old and still cross-legged,
as if learning how to pray.

emerging adulthood

god catches on my teeth and gets stuck in my molars as i
go up the escalator through bakerloo's esophagus, choked
up into the kind of thursday with an unfinished
face. i want to ask my mother
why she made me, if she ever imagined
me collecting all my selves from the five o'clock shadows
that open in the streets like thighs, more out of instinct
than desire. the days
sit on me like sweat-wet sheets and
time watches me
taste the colors change in people's faces, i can feel
god's breath, drying my skin, losing patience.

Park Joon
초복

　동네 사람들에게는 토종닭을 주고 타지 사람들에게는 미리
풀어놓은 폐계를 잡아 주던 삼거리 닭집 진용이네
같은 반을 하는 내내 도시락 반찬으로 닭고기를 싸 오던 진용이는
닭이 물리지 않는다고 했다

　미용을 배우던 진용이는 일찍 동네를 떠났고 배달을 도맡아
하던 진용이네 아주머니는 두 해 전 초복, 빗길
위에서 오토바이를 몰다 떠났다

　자주 취해 있던 진용이네 아저씨는 나를 알아보지 못 했는지
토종닭을 구별하지 못했는지 간혹 내게 폐계를
주었다

　한번은 사 온 닭을 전기솥으로 삶은 적도 있었다 뜸이 들다가도
보온으로 넘어가는 전기솥 탓일까 혹은 그날도
폐계를 받아 온 것일까 닭은 밑도 없이 질겼다 이제 전기솥은 고칠
만한 곳을 찾지 못하면 버릴 만한 날을 찾을
것이다

　설익은 밥을 물에 말아 먹는 것으로 복달임을 대신한다
진용이는 인천 어디에 있다는 미용실에서 백숙처럼
흰 손으로 사람의 머리털을 자르고 있을 것이다 한참을
자르다가도 멈춰 서서 이 여름 저녁으로 밀려드는 질긴
것들을 물끄러미 바라볼 것이다

Originally published in *We May See the Rainy Season Together* by Moonji
Publishing Co., Ltd.

Early Mid-Summer

Jinyong's parents owned a chicken restaurant at the intersection, served local chicken to villagers and aged chicken to visitors. When we were in the same class, Jinyong brought chicken for lunch every day. He said he never got sick of chicken.

Jinyong trained as a hairdresser, left the neighborhood early. His mother who'd been in charge of the delivery died two years ago driving her motorcycle on a rainy road.

Jinyong's father was often drunk. He either didn't recognize me or couldn't tell a local chicken from an aged one and sometimes sold me aged chicken.

One time I steamed the chicken in a pressure cooker. Maybe it was because of the insulation or I got another aged chicken that day, but it was extremely tough. Now the pot is waiting to be disposed of unless I find a place that can fix it.

Instead of having hot soup to relieve the summer heat, I eat undercooked rice dumped in hot water. Fingers white as boiled chicken, Jinyong must be cutting human hair at a salon somewhere in Incheon. He'll cut for a while then pause to stare at the tough things rolling into this summer evening.

처서

앞집에 살던 염장이는
평소 도장을 파면서 생계를 이어가다
사람이 죽어야 집 밖으로 나왔다

죽은 사람이 입던 옷들을 가져와
지붕에 빨아 너는 것도 그의 일이었다

바람이 많이 불던 날에는
속옷이며 광목 셔츠 같은 것들이
우리가 살던 집 마당으로 날아 들어왔다

마루로 나와 앉은 당신과 나는
희고 붉고 검고 하던 그 옷들의 색을
눈에 넣으며 여름의 끝을 보냈다

Originally published in *We May See the Rainy Season Together* by Moonji
Publishing Co., Ltd.

End of Summer

The mortician who lived across the street
made a living carving stamps and
only left his house when someone died.

It was also his job to wash the clothes of the deceased,
hang them on the rooftop.

On windy days
underwear and cotton shirts
flew into our yard.

Sitting on the porch, you and I
fixed the white, red, black of those clothes into our eyes
as we spent the last of the summer.

Will Neuenfeldt
Extra

Every day is another scene on plastic benches with
prop newspapers while two leads take turns on the tire swing.
Sometimes forty dollars isn't worth it so I avoid the set altogether
and sneak across back lots before stumbling into one more role.
Two hooded men pull off the slick bank heist yet
hesitate to recite their next lines because I cut into the long take.
Chewed out by the director, I'm still handed a check.
Another late lunch some fry cook reheats a burger for me.
Sure beats the days I'd cater cast members without costumes
and a single thank you as I refilled scrambled eggs for minimum wage.
Back at the apartment the door is shut and I cut to lopsided cushions
to tune into today's scene with me in the background of Hollywood dreams.

Mia Lindenburg
3rd and Pine

We're walking past the McDonald's on the corner
where we can always score
the one even the tourists know to ignore

and we see the same old,
tired,
ragged faces there.

It seems odd that in the midst of all this natural majesty
there'd be such sadness here.

Maybe it's the rain, like all the jokes say,
drowning us slowly
and flooding algae, dirt, and sewage out

It could be the sun,
the lack thereof,
but Nordic Heritage taught us to stock up on fish oil

I wonder if it's the way the mountain looms over us,
teasing her crooked smile,
just far enough away to remind us how low we are

Or maybe some part of us is left blistered still,
like the loggers we were before,
rolling our wares down Skid Row.

Whatever it is, it's reason enough to climb up Cap Hill,
just to wander around drinking half empties off Broadway

and meet up with friends we hate,
smiling because they get us what we love.

I get so sick of it all sometimes,
waking up to swear we won't do this again,
and then finding ourselves back here.

I don't know if I hate this city,
or just hate who I am in it.

Either way, I'm ready to damn it all.

But as the morning shakes us out of haze into fog,
we'll settle past forest onto rocky beach,
and the sunrise on the water
will dance for us

speaking of salmon and orcas and seal
and we remember that if we can numb our feelings,
the sound isn't so freezing at all.

Whitney Schmidt

When You Let Yourself Remember

Each summons the next

as a trick handkerchief
from the illusionist's pocket:

a tether of befores and afters
strung together in tight knots
tumbling into light.

They slither out
silky quick, slick and slack,
to puddle on carpet
an infinite pool

a satiny nightgown he lifts
over your head and tosses
carelessly to corners
to steal your breath and catch
your eye as his skin covers

yours. You count folds of blue
waves on endless
oceans of nowhere and not-here
while fabric of his open pants
chafes your thighs into pink

marshmallows. You chew
your tongue so screams never
fall out, unraveling.
You make a fist, make a mouth

with your thumb and finger and press
the first limp edge back inside, then
next and next until you've

swallowed it all and *Abracadabra!*
you open your hand.

Empty.

Do not

let your silence convince you
the illusionist's world is real.

It's only a trick after all.
Truth was always already
tumbling out, just as you are

falling now out of the pocket
of today into yesterdays all knotted
up in endless processions of color.
Do not let yourself get tangled

in thirty years of knots.
Do not be ashamed
your body twitches away when
someone brushes the edge of
you. Let bruises

hurt. Let nightmares
haunt and horrify. They are only
souvenirs, tokens and traces,
faulty synapses firing
past into present.

Now you see clearly,
grab the chain's end
drape the silk around you
let memories fly

flags, badges, blue ribbons.
Be proud of your scraps. Carry them
gently. They held you back

once. Now you hold them.
Look. Your hands are
full.

Scars

My body
is a galaxy
     of illiterate
     wounds
shaped like open-
voweled stars
     scattered
on the canvas
sky of me.

Look   carefully.
     You may see
constellations
of anger
burning   bleak
     and far away.

Lawrence Bridges

Hard Living

The pond and speckled light
encountered as a frame for echoes.
Everything after that is fixed.
Everything before it formless,
open space with no physics.
Landscape is a thin placeholder
for a layer of anything,
like this landscape,
after we answer the question
what is this landscape like?
I started arbitrarily, having
no subject due to hard living,
could picture nothing other than
a picture sent by a friend
who lives in San Francisco near
Golden Gate Park. All
possible frames vibrate,
emanate hurling rectangles
of feedback. I've never visited
this pond. I live entirely
by another's mind when
I have nothing framed of my own.

Karoline von Günderrode

Melete

An Melete

Schüze, o sinnende Muse! mir gnädig die ärmlichen Blätter!
Fülle des Lorbeers bringt reichlich der lauere Süd,
Aber den Norden umziehn die Stürme und eisichte Regen;
Sparsamer sprießen empor Blüthen aus dürftiger Aue.

translated from German by Alani Rosa Hicks-Bartlett

Melete

To Melete

Kindly protect, Oh pensive Muse, my humble leaves!
The balmy southern wind abets the laurel's abundance,
But storms and the iciest rains sweep the north;
Flowers bloom more sparingly from the poorer meadow.

Der Kuß im Traume, aus einem ungedruckten Romane

Es hat ein Kuß mir Leben eingehaucht,
Gestillet meines Busens tiefstes Schmachten,
Komm, Dunkelheit! mich traulich zu Schüze
Daß neue Wonne meine Lippe saugt.

In Träume war solch Leben eingetaucht,
Drum leb' ich, ewig Träume zu betrachten,
Kann aller andern Freuden Glanz verachten,
Weil nur die Nacht so süßen Balsam haucht.

Der Tag ist karg an liebesüßen Wonnen,
Es schmerzt mich seines Lichtes eitles Prangen
Und mich verzehren seiner Sonne Gluthen.
Drum birg dich Aug' dem Glanze irr'dscher Sonnen!
Hüll' dich in Nacht, sie stillet dein Verlangen
Und heilt den Schmerz, wie Lethes kühle Fluthen.

The Kiss in a Dream, From an Unpublished Novel

A kiss has breathed life into me,
Soothed my bosom's deepest yearning,
Come, darkness! Enfold me in sweet stillness
So that my lip can drink new pleasures.

Such a life was immersed in dreams,
And so I live to contemplate dreams forever,
I can loathe the brilliance of all other delights,
Because only the night exhales such a sweet balm.

The day is barren of love-sweet pleasures,
I am pained by the vain resplendence of its light
And I am consumed by the blaze of its sun.
So shield your eyes from the brilliance of earthly suns!
Envelop yourself in the night, it quenches your desire
And heals the pain, like the cool waters of Lethe.

Chen Poyu
名聲的考證

關於名聲的神經痛不時發作。

當雨刷晃過視野，當毛球卡入外套拉鍊。

痛苦的形狀像一棵遭到雷殛的樹。

然後在檢討人際關係之外他開始思考名聲。

「名聲是一隻蜜蜂。」艾蜜莉．狄金生的句子。

想得太多對雙方都沒有好處。

幸運的絲線就像電話線這種古老的發明很可惜是會燒斷的。

蜜蜂透過八字形的舞蹈將訊息轉知其他成員。

關於有花粉的花，水源，新巢址的位置方向與距離。

倒楣遵守固定的原則而他亦步亦趨。可惡，拉鍊又卡住了。

「名聲是易變質的食物。」還是艾蜜莉．狄金生。

狄金生小姐您到底有多在意名聲。

思考一事往往能將注意力移往他處。

就像隱喻的行進。

就像累累的葡萄日日豐碩。

Meditation on Fame

From time to time, the neuralgic pain about fame returns.

When the rain distorts vision, when fuzz balls snag a jacket zip.

The pain is shaped like a lightning-struck tree.

After rethinking interpersonal relationships, he deliberates on fame.

Fame is a bee, wrote Emily Dickinson.

Overthinking doesn't bring anyone any good.

Lucky strings will sadly be burnt like other old inventions, such as the
   telephone cords.

The bees perform a waggle dance to exchange information with each other.

About pollinated flowers, waterhead, sites of new hives and how far they are.

Down on his luck, he follows the rules at every step. Damn, the zip jams again

Again, Dickinson wrote, *Fame is a fickle food.*

How much does she indeed care about fame.

Thinking helps him distract himself.

Like a metaphor coming forward.

就像酒神的花環如果你感興趣。

僅僅十首詩在生前得以出版。

狄金生小姐用絲線將寫在各種紙片上的詩作縫成厚厚的書稿。

一千八百多首，她獨特的筆跡像某種傾斜的舞蹈。

傾斜的押韻與隱喻；還有許多美麗的押花。

有趣的事實：蜂蜜其實不算是易變質的食物。

但他得留意葡萄是否結霜。

所有的電話亭都在一步之遙。

先確定了神經痛是不需要看醫生的那種。

就欣賞痛苦雷殛的樹背景的晚霞。

那顏色是黑紅與淺黃。

Like a colony of grapes growing plumper each day.

Like a wreath that crowns Dionysus, if you will.

A mere ten poems were published in her lifetime.

Dickinson handsewed paper scraps of poems into a hefty manuscript with strings.

1,800 poems and more. Her peculiar handwriting, a dance that slants.

Slant rhymes and metaphors, charming pressed flowers.

Funny thing is, honey isn't exactly a fickle food.

And the grapes, he has to check if they survive the frost.

All telephone booths are within a stone's throw.

But let's make sure the neuralgic pain requires no medical opinion first.

Then watch the sunset glow behind the tree bruised by lightning.

Its dark crimson, its yellow bleached.

願意的五月

淺綠，窗玻璃因為樹淺綠
細小，鳥因為窗玻璃細小
願意的五月，趴在很好的寫字桌
信紙上蓋上光與窗花的浮水印

打開窗，演奏鋼琴打開琴蓋
室內外通風時鳥也可以演唱《詩人之戀》

你的手捏著筆，捏著詩
詩捏著戀愛。願意的五月把信捏成樂團

寫字桌上淺綠的立扇
（曖昧，句子因為窗花曖昧）
紙隨著它浮起來、落下來
你細小地流著汗。戀愛是枚很好的浮水印

在淺綠細小的曖昧中
有一隻小鳥告知了不回答的六月

May is the Month for Willingness

Pale green, a glass window goes pale green because of the trees
Small, a bird goes small because of the window
May is the month for willingness. It leans over a refined writing desk
The letter sheet is stamped with a watermark of light and window grilles

Open the window, open the piano's lid before the playing begins
Fresh air comes in. The bird is chirping *A Poet's Love*

You are holding a pen, a poem
And the poem holds love. The willing May turns the letter into a symphony

On the writing desk, a pale green fan stands
(Ambiguous, sentences ambiguate because of the window grilles)
A sheet of paper floats and sinks with the moving air
Your sweat drips in small beads. Love makes a refined watermark

In small pale green ambiguities
A bird has spoken to the unanswering June

Guy D'Annolfo

Our feat of imagination

Is that an antelope in a costume? My son picks up a picture of Whitman,
with a wired beard, scrunches his brow then emphasizes: *a lot.*
I add, conspiratorially, *it is.* He scrutinizes my expression
for a missing smile. *He's also,* I add, *any various number*

of birds, a zebra, an ostrich, even a tree and a rock,
all under the shadow of that great big multitudinous hat.
He smiles: *you're crazier than me, Dada.* I add, *we're equal crazy;*
you want me to read you one of his poems? He walks away.

You pause at the edge of the darkened bedroom when I return from surgery,
wide eyed at my stubbles, and inability to turn to fully see you.
Is that a scarf around your neck? To cover the staples and tubes, *yeah.*

The costume is complete when I pick up Percy Jackson for our bedtime
reading, which says: we're normal as four nights ago. We're not, though
imagining so heals us. You climb on the bed. We find a safe way to hug.

Unwoven loom

No one asked *where the fuck have you been*
      when Odysseus washed up ten years
          late
      from the Trojan war.

Penelope's mind surely wasn't consumed
      by Laestrygonians, couldn't be
          lulled
      by Siren song.

She too loomed fiction with holes, her weapon
      paused time, the shroud
          unwove
      suitors' action.

No one heard her silent threaded
      story that wove a web
          across
      the infidelities of time.

Lina Odeh

A Thousand Flowers

Once,
I wanted a piano.
Big, keys in a tint of gray –
just like the one mom used to play.
I'd place it by the window that I always keep open,
The one where the most sunlight usually breaks in.
And there I would learn the prettiest of tunes and
practice until the sun is replaced by the moon.
But I guess it's "too difficult", Right?...
The piano? …
-   "How about an acoustic guitar?"
-   "Sure, it sounds fine. It'll fit in the car."
The strings were metal and not as smooth,
but they weren't the problem if I'm telling the truth.
I've learned a couple of songs, before I was through,
because what I really wanted,
I always knew.

Once,
I wanted a sewing machine,
I'd dress myself in the brightest of colors, and
make so much noise, annoy my brothers.
I would make a dress, a shirt, even a skirt. And if I
treat it with caution I would never get hurt!
But still, it's "too dangerous", right?...
The sewing machine?...
"How about a sewing kit?"
I did enjoy that but only for a bit.
maybe if I embroider a hundred tiny flowers…

and so that I tried for a couple of hours, but
I only did a few, because what I really wanted,
I always knew.

…

Once I got everything I needed
And for what I wanted, I never pleaded.

Once I tried to sugar coat,
Rock-hard cotton candies up my throat.

Once I tried to go with the flow,
Like a dead little fish in a sad floating row.

…

And one day
I'll get a shiny little thing, and
hear a sound with a fallacious ring.
It will pop a terrifying question.
And will God help me spill an objection? like:
"I want an ocean under my Clair De Lune
And not just the fraction of your lagoon!"
-   "She doesn't know what she's saying, forgive her!
She likes the strings, and her hands, anyway, shiver -"
-   "In your affection, I am showered,
but even if I stich you a Thousand flowers,
they'd all be stitched in blue.
Because what I want,
I always knew."

Akhmet Baitursynuly

Ат

Сен неге, тұлпар атым! Кісінейсің?
Жабығыб неден көңілің, түсді еңсең?
Ерігіб, ауыздығың қарш-қарш шайнаб,
Бұ қалай, бұрынғыдай сілкінбейсің?

Әлде мен, бабың тауыб, бақпадым-ба?!
Болмаса, жемнен қысыб, сақтадым-ба?
Әйтбесе, әбзелдерің сәнді емес пе?
Жібектен тізгініңді тақпадым-ба?
Малдырыб саф алтынға үзеңгіңді,
Тағаңды шын күмістен қақпадым-ба?

Жауабы иесіне берген атдың:
«Сұрайсың не сәбебден мен жабықтым,
Алыстан құлағыма келер дүбір
һәм дауысы керней тартыб, атқан оқдың.

Кісінеб себебім сол мен аһ ұрған:
Көб жүріб далада енді сейіл құрман.
Әбзелмен жарқыраған әсем басыб,
Аз қалды сыйлы, сынды күндер тұрған.

Жақында жаны ашымас жау кеб шабар;
Қалдырмай әбзелімнің бәрін тонар;
Соқтырған шын күмістен тағаларды;
Сұуырыб айағымнан, олжаланар.

Күйзеліб, жаным ашыб, ауырыб бек,
Қайғырыб, уайым ғыб, тұрмын жүдеб;
Орнына желбуиштің терінді әкеб,
Терлеген бүйіріме жабады деб».

Horse

My steed, why do you whinny?
Why does your head hang?
Restless, mouth chomping at the bit,
Why this, your mane unshaken?

Did I not tend to you?
Did I not feed and protect you?
Did I not praise your beautiful saddle?
Did I not tie your silk reins?
Your gilt stirrups and silver horseshoes,
Did I not hammer them?

The horse gives its sad answer:
"You ask why I frown?
My ears hear hooves approach from afar,
Horns blowing, bullets firing.

Why I whinny and sigh,
Days of strolling in fields are few.
Even adorned with glittering saddle,
I feel respect and beauty dwindle.

The unsouring enemy may soon attack,
May soon take everything from me,
May plunder the hammered silver
Horseshoes from my feet.

I'm worn thin: Broken down, soul-bared,
Ill, grieved, distressed.
I fear that instead of your blanket,
Your cold hide will be what covers
My sweating sides."

B.A. Van Sise
Cavalleria Rusticana

Zoppica sulla gamba destra. C'è
una pallottola blu sepolta perché,
afferma, vale la pena morire per lo Stato,
vale la pena provare. ma in questo momento

c'è rumore, rumore profumato,
sulla strada per il teatro dell'opera
verso il quale sta barcollando così velocemente
che non riesco a stargli dietro.

Ha fatto una figlia, e lei
ha fatto un figlio, e
finalmente c'è qualcuno
che vale la pena trascinare per vederlo,
il migliore che sia:

Cavalleria Rusticana. Il grande vanto
dei brutti tempi: che tutto questo è in qualche modo
nobile, che puoi mettere un bambino
in un papillon e che il mondo intero

si inchinerà mentre abbatti una pergola di papponi,
mondane, ladruncoli, sodomiti, uomini
mezzosepolti sotterrandosi nelle pattumiere
o mendicando mentre passi, per vedere la storia

di quando gli uomini erano uomini, e le donne
erano donne, e tutti erano italiani.
Non ci sono posti peggiori del tuo,
l'angolo in fondo all'ultima fila,

translated from Italian by Eleanora Foglia

Rustic Chivalry

He limps on his right leg. There's
a blue bullet buried in it because,
he states, The State is worth dying for,
worth trying for, but right now

there's noise, perfumed noise,
on the way to the opera house
to which he is wobbling so fast
that I cannot keep up.

He made a daughter, and she
made a son, and
finally there is
someone worth dragging to see it,
it, the best one it is:

Cavalleria Rusticana. The big boast
of bad times: that all of this is somehow
noble, that you can put a little boy
in a bow tie and that the whole world will bow

as you barrel down a bowery of pimps,
tricks, muggers, buggerers, half-buried
men burying themselves in garbage bins
or begging as you go past to see the story

of when men were men, and women
were women, and everyone was Italian.
There are no worse seats than yours,
the back corner of the back row,

e lui si strofina la gamba, finalmente felice
di mettere il passato davanti a sé,
di sedersi in tempi migliori, di sapere
che un mondo si chiude quando si apre un sipario.

and he rubs his leg, finally happy
to put the past ahead of him, to
sit in better times, to know
a world closes when a curtain opens.

A. J. Bermudez
Missing

You live in this table, invisibly
streaked with the oil from your hands.

Your breath is in the walls, married
to powdered plaster and egg white lustre.

The light from this same sun is blinding
you, someplace else.

You are in the air that blows across
the strait.

Somewhere, beneath your feet, on another continent, you
stand and the dust moves for you.

Eugene Datta
The Spot

He was a friend's namesake

and sat with his back against the wall of St. Michael's/
St. Dimitrios Church on Jesuitenstraße –

at the same spot on the sidewalk
for the six or so years that I'd known him,
in good weather and bad.

We spoke every time I stopped

to drop a coin or two in his Starbucks coffee cup –
sometimes just a *hello* and a *thank-you*,

a *you're-welcome* and a *have-a-good-day/weekend*.
Sometimes he'd ask about my children – *All well?*
Enjoying school? Looking forward to (or Enjoyed) the holidays?

He spoke to many others –

the church he had his back to reflected on the glass façade
across the yard in front of him –

blond hair, blue eyes, and gentle
like the one whose namesake he was. It's good to give
to both charity and individuals, he'd said to me once.

The charities do a lot but sometimes we have other needs.

His need at the time was to raise enough money
for a driver's license, so that he could look for a job –

you couldn't get one without that, he said. *No, I don't need
any clothes, thank you!* – head tilted to a side, eyes
squinting, one more tightly against the light than the other.

Why was he on the street? *Long story*, he said.

Someone who looked like he could be the custodian
of the once-Jesuit and now-Greek (Catholic-somewhen-

in-between) church wore black clothes and a black docker hat –
he sat close by on the steps of the church, or stood there,
watching sunlight and shadow strike endless poses in front of him,

leaning into each other like tango dancers.

I'd never seen the two men speak,
but they must have known each other well.

The seasons changed, and with them the angle of light
that filled the open yard, which filled with and emptied of
school children every weekday –

the daily ebb and flow of life my friend's namesake witnessed

from his more-or-less fixed point of view.
His hair grew long and thin, his face wrinkled and shrank.

He looked like he'd given up on the driver's license.
Often, walking past him, I'd catch a whiff of weed in the air.
One day, he wasn't in his place on the sidewalk

and approached me from another side of the street –

could I spare something? I couldn't – I didn't have my wallet
on me; no change in my pocket, either.

He'd never *asked* for money before and never since,
always letting his paper cup do the job for him. That I couldn't
offer anything that day hadn't changed the way he smiled.

Then Covid came.

Familiar faces disappeared behind the strangeness of masks
if they didn't disappear altogether.

Gesund bleiben, he said to me often. You, too, I'd tell him.
He sat there wearing a surgical mask,
maintaining his distance.

The pandemic was nearing its end – there was hope

of life soon returning to normal. In that climate of relief
it occurred to me one day

that the spot on the sidewalk had been empty for weeks.
Then I found someone else sitting there. Dropping a coin
in his cup, I asked if he knew the one who sat there before.

He's dead, the man said.

I didn't ask his name.
I saw him several times. We exchanged greetings.

Take good care of yourself, I'd tell him. Yes, of course, he'd say.
You too! After some time, he didn't sit there anymore.
I never saw him again.

And I never found out what had happened to *him*.

Since then I've seen at least two men occupying that place —
I haven't asked either of them any question.

I don't know if the man in the black docker hat
really was the church custodian — I haven't seen him in months,
although on good days, sunlight and shadow still dance

their slow noontime tango at the same spot.

Helen Steenhuis

Bird without Flight

I lost my voice when I saw the bird on the road,
its wings shattered, a mast with no sail.
The sky was a pool ruffled and vacant, sunless and vast.
It lay quivering, a ball of loosened feathers
stirring under a tepid wind that swept down
to turn the bird onto its side.
There was a flicker, a longing to take flight,
the instinct to move, to go anywhere,
directionless, silently resolute,
to be lifted above the gravelled road.
When will the voice come back
and what will it say —
I have seen the tragedy of the bird without flight.

David Romanda

The Fortune Teller Shuffles Her Cards

What would you like to know? she asks me.
Will I die young?
That's not the sort of question you want to ask.
That's my question.
Excuse me for saying so, but you're no longer young.

VISCERAL, VELOCITIES

Florence Weinberger
Karen Lozinski
Aviva Betzer
Marisa Vito
Yakoub Mousli
S. T. Brant
T.W. Sia
Remon Badan
Riley Mayes
Naomi Leimsider
Laine Derr

Florence Weinberger

Through Which a Visceral Language Materializes

I knew you would argue dolphins, so blatant
their emanations, but you'd never guess radiant windows

is how I know my neighbor's reconciliations.
The waver of leaves as I water at the root is found speech,

I speak charity for the ragged running rabbit stalked
by a voracious hawk, my soul in tatters taught grace.

Maybe you faced corn husks singing like demented tenors
the corn is as high as an elephant's eye

and entered that rare atmosphere, where your body began
to run out of words.

Not all endeavor is holy. Often prayer strays toward gold,
confession ends in lame excuses,

and even when you profess, you shrink your mistakes
down to the size of a spitball.

The Big One, the psychically subconscious half-willful
dumb mistake you made

when you weren't that young, the journal you filled
with every indiscreet thing you ever did

and now you can't discard without reading first, without
the urge to keep turning the pages, inflicting on yourself

the maim of revived memory;
what will you do for expiation, pray? Send a check

to the trenches? Bend from the waist? Instead,
try entering a synagogue the final hours of Yom Kippur,

the congregation famished from fasting, and attend
to the sound of the shofar, the ram's horn that once

warned of war, brought news of celebration, summoned
the tribes to waken and rise to what some call the Divine,

and tell me the hair on the nape of your neck didn't bristle.
Or stand transfixed in an alley

in the old city in Jerusalem next to an open door
beside a church bruised by centuries,

the limpid notes of a young girl singing a cappella
an ancient Gregorian chant drifting onto the worn stones,

and try to hold back your tears.
Listen to the twined voices of the muezzin

chanting from the minarets in Istanbul, bring in to yourself
the weave of brio, body and bamboo

in the hands of a shakuhachi player, find a language for
Louis Armstrong, Miles Davis, Wynton Marsalis

hallowing the air the way Beethoven's Ninth sanctified
the Nineteenth Century, and Presley, Pavarotti, Callas,

have blessed ours. It is possible to feel the earth thrill,
to retrieve our animal vocabulary.

Karen Lozinski
Cusp of Nocturne

Day splinters into sequins
sticky gold wraps laminate blood orange
and know-it-all pink
hues tossed through a tangle of crepe myrtle
branches frilled purple and white
dampened to shadow and silhouette.
It's okay to rest even if your skin won't let you
The squirrel frogs who shelter in
the shell ginger as diurnal citadel
throw their voices into coming darkness
rejoicing in the recent rains
like the scraping of a thousand happy guiros
Let this chorus create a current of contentment
Roost-ready cardinals swoop through
stitch the grey air with carmine flourish
claim their constellations in push pin chirps
hopping from holly to ligustrum to camellia
every limb is home, but only one is for dreaming
These rituals and rhythms are within your grasp
My soul stirs its way up to the limits of skin
corpuscles sing with oxygen and ecstasy
synapses a conflagration, nervous system crackles
can barely contain the lightning within
I gather the indigo curtain of night
its patterns a resplendence of infinity
and dash into what I already know
striving to unlock what I don't
A sacred chaos can birth its own bliss

Aviva Betzer
SOS

I circle you, a bitch sniffing for ink. Like Medusa
I write in blood, milk, chalk
I kill people with my eye yet
I wish I were dead.
I hold on to routine, terrified of nights.
I pick at the wound, my daily bread.
I write to my friends:
The car broke down, there's a power cut, the water's off.
Talking to you is a bomb.
I think I may have been you in another life.

Dark Journey

I travel along with dull pebbles
In my mouth. I hang on to daydreams
And it takes
Me six minutes to choose an outfit
And six hours to think think think
Seeing through the window
The passing of darker recollections
Of this journey, inside my head.
I am catapulted by words
I no longer contain.

Marisa Vito
Me and The Salt

When you go to the aquarium, the staff teach you how to pet fish.
Fish must be touched with two fingers and gently stroked. The fish are
scared, but are open to being touched. Sometimes people would roughly
poke at the fish, not caring about the two finger rule. I also ignored the
two finger rule; grazing the fish using one finger.

I thought the fish were fine with me petting them with my index alone.
But imagine,
feeling one finger when you were expecting two.

$$\sim$$

The whale one, her favorite story.
      I enjoyed watching her talk, watching her turn old.
      She told me she loved Moby Dick and Asian girls.

$$\sim$$

At night, she burned kerosene
to keep us from being in the dark,
outlined by how our bodies swam around each other.

She rubbed her hands against mine
and I thought how can anyone be afraid of this?
Her nose moved against my zones of skin and attachment.

I began to feel my eel egg heart squirming and hatching itself,
under the pressure of her fist, opening and closing inside of me.

~

I believe in what I fail at
        and this time, it was my own pedagogy,
        my dedication to the love plot.

I craved wanton wantedness, the selfish memory of sex, her face smoothing
the surface of mine.

Now, I want different language, honest language.

~

Violence and intimacy always coexist   there is this feeling spectrum.
                        In the middle is fantasy
I don't know what she was thinking   when she raped me.

                I was thinking that love is magic—
                it is the ointment and the cause.

~

My little ritual of

mopping my pubic hairs off her tongue.

No one likes hair in their mouth
and it is embarrassing how wiry my hair is.

My vagina sore, swollen, and red,
I would turn away from her
and hate myself.

Rape is tiring.
Queer rape is alienating.

Maybe I am lucky
I can drift alone on top of the ship planks,
waiting for someone to find me

and yell "Marisa!
Is that you? Marisa!
How long have you been out here?"

Until that happens, it is me
and the salt pouring itself over
my bodily autonomy.

No one asking how
the ship sank.

~

The sea gifts its little bones on the edges of its sweaty knees. I always took them home and put them in my seashell box, to remember the ocean and its body.

Rape was a seashell placed by my feet. I took it because that is what one does, when given something. I bit into the seashell, cracking my jaw, my tongue a blood seal. I was searching for the tiny grains of sand between my teeth, hearing them rub together. Only I can hear the crunch of time, the pebbled touch of loss.

Yakoub Mousli

IV In the Shadow of Salieri

I drank from my soul before I poured it into words,
Ah! Such sweet bitter nectar.

Silence spoke through the splinters of time
When time was all there was,
Idly comforting my long-lasting solitude, he said—
Well... who remembers what said he, it does not matter,
He does not matter, for he's always around, and I, I
Too, am always around.
Here, in the black nest of solitude
While pen drips my blood into these pages,
Bright, fluid, into these pages, for a glimpse,
Only,
As it swiftly turns rotten.
Though seldom, though swift; upon reading,
These words, they rush, and we, we live again.
These precious rotten heaps fermented a lifetime
Now crawl onto my frail legs,
Sustained, only, by beauty.
Ah, yes, so he spoke, "Show me a shred a beauty,
And I'll give you a full, bursting heart."
Alas, companion, like all others you are;
Beauty, here, around us; though dark,
Though rotten of kind, still,
You fail to see.

There is a galaxy within me, and within me
Sprouts through all that which is unknown.
And gave it, did I, I gave it all throughout my time

As my breast expanded, more, more;
All trifling and vain, yet, still,
I am what makes me more, and I am what makes me less.
I, barefoot and hungry, have roamed the cosmos,
And fashioned words out of stars, and spread them;
Nebulae, who's beauty the Angels covet.
Yet my path of roaming entranced me, ravished me to love
To lose and to suffer —and all I loved, I loved alone,
And all I suffer, I suffer alone.
Love? Ah! Yes, Love.
How did my blood flow for it once?
Here! I'm sure it is here.
Yes.
"Those who feel the most love the hardest,
Those who love the hardest, love not themselves.
Those, who love not themselves, love not one another."
~~Those who feel the most love the hardest,~~
~~Those who love the hardest, love not themselves.~~
~~Those, who love not themselves, love not one another.~~
Rubbish.

I, in my darkness, lay unhinged.
With the single scent of all my years.
With the shadow that lurks around me.
With the shadow that lurks around me!
The shadow which lurks in the shadows?
The sha…
Is …
I die?
I DIE! I DIE! DIE! DIE! I DIE!
AT LAST, OLD FRIEND, YOU'VE COME, HERE, I DIE!
COME, SIT, POUR COFFEE, LET US CONVERSE.
LET ME HEAR YOU, I BEG, AT LEAST FOR A BREATH.
I'VE LISTENED FOR YOU, A MYRIAD BEFORE.
TELL ME, I BEG, OF HOW MUCH YOU CRAVED ME,

OF HOW MUCH YOU'VE YEARNED, TO TOUCH,
TO SIT BY ME, BUT COULDN'T BEFORE.
DIE! I DIE! AT LAST, I DIE!
LET US REJOICE. At last, I die!
—   — — —

You're not there, are you?
No.
Silence; — — — —
— — — — — — — —
— — — — — — —
— — — — — — — —
— — — — — —
— — — — — —

My path of roaming entranced me, ravished me and left me bare
Where two roads diverged in a wood, and I—
I took the one less traveled by,
And knew why people shunned it.

S. T. Brant
Chaos is a Melody (Here is how the Lovers Meet)

The Garden of Memory is a garden of music.
Music as vicious as it's sweet. Did you learn nothing
On the water? You would linger on the mountains
Of delight, having learned nothing on the water.

Your feet stay planted to the ground,
So you mistake the rockfall for a mountain,
Not noticing all that's passing. Pleasure is a landslide
To Averno. Will you be of the fall, in the path?

Do you not remember the beautiful singing from before?
When you walked in the clear night of old times
With no clouds to coat the stars or moon, no modesty
Of time, no formality with you, simply the revelations

Of the heart introducing its new moments to its old,
The wedding bells in you, your soul the busy toller,
Announcing the communion of all time to Now,
It's all with you always. Yet you are at the roadside

Awaiting the circus of annulment to run by, to offer you
Employment, opportunity, to grant you some chaos
Where all living is a burning, hot wretchedness
That feels pleasurable because it is the first fountain

You've encountered of that water, a dazzling wellspring
Never seen but by those in this procession, these new angels,
Angels of fresh and tireless experience. They are angels
Yoked to dissonance, can't you hear the minor key

That's cutting up this melody? God plays a demon's harp,
Counterpoints Love's song. I sing you ways to love
And carry on. Listen! What is chaos that you want?
You learned nothing from the waves, amorphous mermaids

Dancing your ship to shore, shoring your vision to an image
You can hold, Aphrodite walking love out of the sea,
You a bubble from her feet bursting into being,
Caught in the arms of melody, singing to you now,

Your head across her knees, her hands running through
Your hair, her song is life to me, she's singing us all free,
Beneath the tree too incandescent for us to see,
A star arboreal, brightness in a shape is all to say, entropy

The fruit that stocks the boughs, red serpents swimming
An aura that offers them an apple sheen.
Do you know what chaos is?
That singing.

The song of how the lovers meet
Blooms persimmons on the cherubims
That hum the fire of the sun
As yard lamps that perpetuate the spring.

My sixth-grade teacher accuses me of trying to kill myself and

I write an apology letter to Pranav for asking
him to watch me go. I start with *I'm sorry*

but I really mean *would you carry my body
home for me?* I have crossed so many lines that

I leave him ▮▮▮▮ with an erasure poem
▮▮▮▮▮▮▮▮▮▮▮▮▮▮▮▮▮▮▮▮

▮▮▮ In the pick-up zone ▮▮▮▮
his mom looks at me ▮▮▮▮ with

eyes ▮▮▮▮▮▮▮▮▮▮▮▮▮▮

A phone call comes in the middle of dinner and my mother asks me
to translate my teacher's voice. I watch her face change ▮▮▮ she
understands me ▮▮▮ hesitating over the language they didn't teach
me in school. She ▮▮▮ takes her kitchen cleaver and puts it in my
hand. *I made you,* ▮▮▮ *I deserve to watch my own animal do it.*

There is a picture that I drew back then. I have our family on an imagined
porch in crayon. In front of our place on Bryant Common. Everything is
right,

even I am missing.

A bottle of expired Advil sits in the bottom drawer of my nightstand. There are maybe 12 pills in there, but I don't keep count. I spent that entire summer ██████████ silent in my blankets.

My mother takes me to the ocean. She dips
a toe in and says *it's too cold.*

She keeps it in anyways.

My mother doesn't ask me why / I spend a lifetime answering her back.

Remon Badan

Gas Money

With my tight grip on a Necromantic pedal,
His voice   floats above the unmarked grounds
of a territorial grandmother, drifting through domestic lands, we fall in and
out of an argumentative strand;   (he and I)
fighting over tensed-up muscles and non-retractable
soul crushers – we drive inside the stomach of the angry Borders.
Struggling to keep our frequ-
                                encies intact, He mimics the Harshness
of the static radio
as it rips—
through our intimate vehicle of time
and reminds us our home is unfamiliar terrain, claimed
by a borderless Medusa.

Eternally she walks the underbelly   of Jerusalem,
returning us back to the fertile soil   of Nativity, where I

am an aging Prophet,
  and he; a migrating Pigeon,

growing forgetful of our domestic burdens,   she eats away at our eyes
screaming: unwelcomed lovers   unwelcomed lovers   unwell-
comed in the heart of a culture of masculine   horror.

Bleeding carbon dioxide,
he can tell we are starting   to lose
our color, Battling ancestral   devils   and a weakened gas pedal,
we slow the pace   down until   we run out
                        of road,
and split the Gas Money.

Riley Mayes

accident 74 on holyrood

there has never been anything but the smoking door,
the smashed pole, the roundabout turned flat by
the rammed body of the delivery truck. upright, at least;
but deflated of all his usual energies: swearing,
cackling, adjusting the sweat brim of his hat to sit
between his temples and above his glasses. the ever-pulling
 presence of time yanking his shoulders towards his ears.
 it was always this job, that he never meant for it to become more
but in fact it was, it was, every node of his life was
connected to this veiny engine, this vessel, now smoking.
bumper wrenched off and lying like a whale's broken jawbone.
yet: nothing has been so simple as the collision.
that momentary jerk, the slip of wrists resting,
turning until the window is white with motion and
let it come slowly upon him, the sailing weightlessness,
the unlatching of time. motion flows through unparticular space,
parting the blood tides of his body, winding through
 his nerves, leaching out the other side of him,
then closing, *snap shut*,
his father's briefcase, his mother's polaroid camera,
metal striking metal and making meat of his car.
airbag inflating like a white, poisonous mushroom,
that hinging of time becoming, at once, forced shut again,
bringing him here, to his moment, where the hex of
his schedule, the normalcy, the routine is
wrenched right through.

Naomi Leimsider

Patient is Now Unable at Multiple Levels (Notes)

Patient is a person who experienced sudden onset consistent with evidence. History has been severe — very severe — the present is what it seems, and the future, as always, is unknown, undetermined: this situation — and perhaps others to come — notwithstanding.

Some function, little function, waning function, absence of function (incomplete may become complete or remain)

After long days of nothing who can say.
How to communicate this: You will now
live in the small space between.

How to explain?

First there was bled out fluid — it trickled, gushed, reabsorbed, trickled again — through the slow flow of malformations in barely visible caverns.

Imagine a vessel traveling through the tangle of bloody networks down expanding paths among lost soft lesions in such spacious places, in immense dark depths, only to find it abandoned, hollowed out, in rapid decline.

Consider a come and go violent injury without violence, a cavernous complex formation followed quickly by degeneration. A complicated incomplete yet complete non-injury injury. Hemorrhagic and sporadic.

You are in need of acute awareness: the divide in understanding is, quite clearly, deep and wide.

Extensive evaluation then prepped with no clear reason
(difficulty obtaining clearance). Struck down by slowness,
out of the bare minimum of luck. Patient introduced to the useless
      universe, the long reach
of time. Did time forget what to do, how to move?

Patient is now unable at multiple levels.

Remember the old adage: A pumped stomach always reveals its contents.
Ask Patient: how do you feel?
Ask Patient: how do you hurt?
Ask Patient: who are you now?

Evidence is extensive, so extensive, but still
we ask: Same, worse, or better? Same, worse, or better?
For more significant revelations ask
specific questions!
But in the end, we rely on summary again and again:
Delicate surgery begets no surgery;
difficult clearance begets no clearance.
Evaluate and evaluate and evaluate,
but do not encourage.
Reassess, reassess, reassess,
then do not bother.
Patient is
unable.
Unable to seek
care
Unable to facilitate
care
Unable to know
who will
care,
do the
caring,

how to
care.

Do Not Share:
Perhaps you have arrived at the last place. Do not think
about other possibilities. You wondered where or when
or how it would come: the time is now. Do not consent:
it shouldn't have happened this way, but you borrowed
time. Hijacked, ransacked, plundered time until the moment,
the very last moment, before unexpected event. Do not
consult: what more could anyone say. What can and
cannot, will and will not, happen next is never known.
Do not consider: none of us can enhance or assess or
reason with chance. Did you listen for the ringing, the
warning shot: you are out of time. This is it. Now. This
is what will take you down.

Laine Derr
Mourning

My sadness
is a thin
layer of skin,
blinds opened
to the morning
sun, I fight its
shimmer, a hum
telling me it's
not raining, but
I know it is,
lashes damp
w/ rays of dew.

OBSERVATIONS

Jon Tadmor
Marianne Moore
Linda Leavell
Cristanne Miller
Dotty LeMieux
Taylor Franson-Thiel
(attributed to) Columba   Christian Lopac
Esther Jansma   Arno Bohlmeijer
Avishag Eliav
James Ph. Kotsybar
Abhishek Udaykumar
Margaret Marcum
Mazzy Sleep
Yolanda Hansen
Tjizembua Tjikuzu
CLS Sandoval
Elaine Verdill
Samantha Malay
Reginald Saint-Vincent Paul
Nina Knueven
B.A. Van Sise   Eleanora Foglia
Luke Carson

Jon Tadmor

Marianne Moore's *Observations* at 100

In the spring of 1934, a senior at Vassar College found herself trawling the library for any anthology or little magazine that would contain another poem by her newest literary obsession – Marianne Moore. Luckily, the college librarian happened to be a childhood acquaintance of the poet. The student later recalled:

> *Miss Borden's copy of* Observations *was an eye-opener in more ways than one. [The poems] struck me, as they still do, as miracles of language and construction. Why had no one ever written about things in this clear and dazzling way before? But at the same time I was astonished to discover that Miss Borden [...] obviously didn't share my liking for these poems.[1]*

Despite her own reticence about the poems, Miss Borden the librarian arranged for the student, herself an aspiring poet, to meet Moore. This would lead to a close artistic and personal relationship between Moore and the young student, Elizabeth Bishop. Moore even shepherded the first appearance of Bishop's poems in a printed anthology about a year after their first meeting.

Fortunately, we no longer need to happen upon one of the poet's acquaintances to find a copy of *Observations* today. This past decade has seen a new edition of *Observations* (2016, ed. Linda Leavell), as well as a meticulously edited *New Collected Poems* (2017, ed. Heather Cass White). These new editions continue to perpetuate readers' interest in Moore's work, alongside recent critical and scholarly projects such as Linda Leavell's 2013 biography *Holding On Upside Down: The Life and Work of Marianne Moore*, the *Marianne Moore Digital Archive* and the anthology *Twenty-First Century Marianne Moore: Essays from a Critical Renaissance* (2018, eds. Elizabeth Gregory & Stacy Carson Hubbard).

As one of those readers whose love for Moore's work was stoked by these recent editions and additions, as someone for whom the first encounter with her poetry ignited a response much like that of Bishop – again, "Why had no one ever written about things in this clear and dazzling way before?" – I knew I had to find some way of paying tribute to this inimitable figure on the centennial of her first collection of poetry. The first years of this third decade were marked by modernist centennials, from *Ulysses* to *The Wasteland*, and *Observations* merits its place right alongside them.

Pedantic literalists will note that *Observations* was technically not Moore's first collection, as her *Poems* had appeared in 1921. At the time, Moore had been publishing poems for several years, but she was not convinced that she has enough material for an entire volume. Her friends, the writers Bryher and H.D., published *Poems* in England without Moore's knowledge or agreement. As Linda Leavell writes in *Holding on Upside Down*, Moore was "furious" not only because of the betrayal of her trust, but "was even angrier that her first book was not the one she wanted."[2] The book she wanted was *Observations*. But even that was not enough, as she published a revised edition shortly thereafter in 1925. She would have another chance to revise the poems, their order, their titles, everything, in 1935 when she put together her *Selected Poems* with T.S. Eliot. The poems of *Observations* would see further revisions at almost any point Moore had a chance to collect her poems: in 1951's *Collected Poems* and in 1967's *Complete Poems*. The latter edition notoriously opens with the epigraph, "Omissions are not accidents." And indeed, at this late stage in her career Moore had no qualms about excising old poems from the supposedly "Complete" collection, changing their titles, or even heavily revising poems, including some of her most beloved works. "Poetry," perhaps her most famous poem, began its life as a five-stanza poem, was immediately reduced to only thirteen lines as early as the 1925 edition of *Observations*, and by 1967 was whittled down to a tercet.

How to pay tribute to a poet whose thinking and writing is constantly on the move? A more important question – how should we let this thinking and writing move us a century later? These were the questions, among many others, that inspired this special section of *Mantis*, commemorating *Observations* at 100. Some of the poems, translations, and essays presented here were directly inspired by Moore herself. Others were included because they spoke to one of the many aspects and values of her work. Included here are also contributions by scholars and editors of Moore whom I would like to acknowledge before we begin (if there is a name for this particular community of Moore aficionados within and without the academy – "The Pedantic Literalists," "The Dodgers," maybe "The Rats"? – please do let me know).

Linda Leavell's poem "Monhegan Island" opens the section with a dazzling tribute in verse. Cristanne Miller's essay, "On Drafting toward *Observations*," gives us a fascinating look inside Moore's notebooks, published by the *Marianne Moore Digital Archive* (https:// moorearchive.org), as she was drafting the poems for inclusion in her first volume. Concluding the section, Luke Carson's essay "*Observations*' Index," provides our second bookend, exploring the strange index Moore attached to the book. Between these bookends, you will find more wonderful new poetry and translations. Some of them engage with Moore directly, but in all of them I hope you will find what she called "a place for the genuine."

[1] Elizabeth Bishop, "Efforts of Affection: A Memoir of Marianne Moore," Prose, ed. Lloyd Schwartz. Farrar, Straus and Giroux, 2011, 118.

[2] Linda Leavell, Holding On Upside Down: The Life and Work of Marianne Moore. Farrar, Straus and Giroux, 2013, 192.

Marianne Moore

To Yvor Winters

       something of a badger-Diogenes –
we are indebted technically; and
attached personally, those of us who know him;
are proud of his hostility to falsity;
of his verse reduced to essence;
of a tenacity unintimidated by circumstance.
He does not hesitate to call others foolish,
and we do not shrink from imputations
of folly – of annoying a man to whom
compliments may be uncongenial;
– wise to be foolish when a sense of indebtedness
is too strong to suppress.

To Yvor Winters -

something of a badger-Diogenes -
we are indebted technically; and
attached personally, those of us who know him;
are proud of his hostility to falsity;
of his verse reduced to essence;
of a tenacity unintimidated by circumstance.
He does not hesitate to call others foolish,
and we do not shrink from imputations
of folly - of annoying a man to whom
compliments may be uncongenial;
- wise to be foolish when a sense of indebtedness
is too strong to suppress.

Marianne Moore

Note:

This is a poem Moore contributed to a special issue of *Sequoia: Stanford Literary Magazine*, published by the Associated Students of Stanford University in Winter 1961. The issue was dedicated to Yvor Winters, the esteemed poet and critic who taught at Stanford's English department since he earned his PhD from that same department in 1934 until his retirement in 1966. Moore and Winters had been acquainted since the 1920s, and he was an early and adamant supporter of her work.

Linda Leavell

Monhegan Island

"Water in motion is far
from level," said the poet who
brought me here.

I climb Ambrose's hill and see his
"not-native books and hat," his
view of the harbor, and keep
going until the fir trees, each
with their "emerald turkey foot,"
mark the edge of the sea.

No one ushers me down the
narrow, unimproved steps
to the granite nook in the cliff
where I find my seat—
protected from the afternoon sun, my neighbors
anonymous insects and tufts
of grass. Below me, the gulls
on their blacker rocks raucously mock
my long absence.

Their tickets to
this "drama of water against
rock" never expire. I come
only for the matinee.

Impossible to paint or
film, the surf pounds the glacier-cut
rocks that won't be subdued

into roundness or sand. No victors here.
The rising green waves cover
the rocks with their
whiteness, their churning swirl, and then
succumb to the pull of the next
swell. Endlessly different but
unchanged for millennia.

Here at the inner wrist of
the earth, I feel
its pulse.

Cristanne Miller
On Drafting toward *Observations*

Many critics have commented on the importance of Walt Whitman's 1855 *Leaves of Grass*, including one who calls it the "single most original book of poetry ever written in the history of the world."[1] T. S. Eliot's 1922 publication of "The Waste Land" has received similar accolades in relation to modern poetry. Marianne Moore's 1924 *Observations* should be recognized similarly as a monumental moment in the history of modern poetry. In *Observations*, Moore takes Whitman's poetic innovation a step further by divorcing syntactic closure and sometimes even word boundaries from the poetic line. Moore combines the apparently arbitrary lineation of prose with the highly stylized formal (syllabic) meter and the precisely patterned rhyme of poetry. Like Eliot, but with greater irony and humor, she attaches the commentary of notes and an index to her volume of poems, spoofing traditions of source-hunting and hierarchical seriousness with her entries. The effect is profoundly democratic and challenging, demanding that we make sense for ourselves of her sometimes puzzling and often witty juxtapositions of description, trenchant commentary, and reflection—mostly in syllabic verse although in the early 1920s she turns to equally remarkable free verse for her longest poems. *Observations* is unique, a landmark of adventurous poetic innovation, cultural commentary, eco-environmental wisdom, understated feminism, and quirky playfulness.

The question of why Moore has received less attention than other poets, for this volume and her entire oeuvre, has been answered in earlier decades but perhaps deserves brief attention again in this centennial year—when we may understand with new clarity the precarity of women's status in the professional world, and generally. While there have been many gains in women's rights and openness to women's achievement over the past century, gender still looms as the primary impediment to Moore's deserved full acknowledgment as being among the most significant innovators of modern verse. I mean this in two ways. First, for all the decades of her own life, most (although definitely not all!) critics and readers were less willing to see radical innovation as stemming from a woman than a man, particularly if that woman followed behavioral characteristics generally regarded as conventional or feminine—and despite Moore's winning every major poetry prize available in the United States: the Pulitzer, Bollingen, National Book Award, Gold Medal of the National Institute of Arts and Letters, and in France the Chevalier de l'Ordre des Arts et des Lettres—among others. Moore did depart from stereotypes of femininity—as Elizabeth Gregory has most recently argued—but those departures were quieter than, for example, Gertrude Stein's.[2]

Second, both male but especially female and feminist readers and critics since the 1970s have sought out earlier poets and stylistic innovators from those whose departures from convention were openly marked in their personal lives: sexually, sartorially, and in their social politics. Not (openly) lesbian, bohemian, or politically radical—despite her feminism and ongoing support for what we now call diversity and equity, and she would have called Civil Rights, Moore lived with her mother until 1947, demanded some degree of decorum, and was relatively soft-spoken. She has seemed, and perhaps to some still seems, an unlikely candidate to be an extraordinary innovator of poetic form or a profound spokesperson for major issues of her century. And yet that is precisely what *Observations* proves her to be, from its brief syllabic verses to its long free-verse poems; from the manifestos of "Poetry, "Roses Only," and "The Labors of Hercules" to the profound musings of "England," "Black Earth," and "In This Age of Hard Trying Nonchalance is Good And." We learn from this volume and see in her life, as Moore writes in "Radical"—a poem spoken in the voice of a carrot—"that which it is impossible to force, it is impossible / to hinder."[3] And as "Radical" and other *Observations* poems indicate, Moore herself was thinking about hierarchies of power and gender as she completed the poems collected in this volume.

There is no record of Moore's drafts of the poems she completed before 1922. For some poems, there are early typed or earlier published and then revised editions—beautifully documented in Robin G. Schulze's *Becoming Marianne Moore: The Early Poems 1907-1924*. Starting in 1922, however, Moore kept a poetry draft notebook, containing what are apparently her earliest drafts for the poems "Marriage," "An Octopus," "Silence," and "Sea Unicorns and Land Unicorns."[4] In 2016, the *Marianne Moore Digital Archive* (*MMDA* https://moorearchive.org/) published this notebook in facing page manuscript and edited, annotated transcription.[5] This notebook allows us both to think in new ways about Moore's process of composition and to reflect on the concerns Moore repeated as she worked toward the final poems of this collection.

This notebook puts to rest the idea, initiated by Moore herself, that she composed by conceiving of a particular syllabic stanza and then organizing other material toward a poem following that pattern. While this may be true of the moment when she begins to move her crafted phrases into syllabic form, Moore's initial composition consists of repeated and reorganized words, phrases, and groups of lines.[6] In this notebook, these phrases with some frequency include an "I" position and pronoun that appears to reflect Moore herself, the kind of personal pronoun she largely edited out of her early verse.[7] Such personal pronouns show a feistiness and emotional engagement easier to overlook in finished poems where the "I" is downplayed or disappears.

This 1922-1930 notebook also suggests a different organization of its initial material than has been supposed, as Moore moves toward the crafted phrases used in published poems. In 1984, Patricia C. Willis argued that in this notebook Moore was drafting a single poem, which she later separated into distinct compositions, trying out two titles for this one poem: "Marriage" and "An Octopus."[8] It seems to me that this notebook instead indicates that Moore from the start conceived of different poems, which she worked on simultaneously, including from one line to the next on the same page. Willis is correct that Moore tries out several phrases, and ideas, without being sure where they will finally be used, if at all. These indeed indicate the connections, for her, among different poems' concerns. Her repeated centering of distinct titles and leap from one subject to another, however, suggest that her initial drafting is rarely toward a single work for long. As ideas or phrases occur to her, for various poems, she jots them down. The first proper page of this notebook (perhaps written late in her drafting) includes:

Marriage   lupin small blue flowers growing
        Mt Rainier   close together so that patches of them
                        looks like sheets of blue water in the distance
Tropics & unicorns   I too am not fickle
                        I too am happy only at home
Peter   see mole's BR Nov 8   fr to enslave
                one meets it, whiskers out
Hermes Bk of Noble Dogs   his robust personality
Peter voluntary curfew half past 2
        My past life has not been a parody on the real
                                    (*MMDA*, 07.04.04: 2)

Later on this page, she writes "neatness of finish, neatness of finish," a phrase near the conclusion of the published "An Octopus" and not recurring in the notebook, although on page 74 she twice writes "niceness of finish."

    As this page indicates, this notebook also includes a few phrases or lines pointing toward "People's Surroundings" (published 1922) and "Peter," first published in *Observations*—although its four references to a "tomcat" or "Tom cat" "& his enemy" (12, 18, 23, 29) occur in the midst of other lines suggesting "Marriage"—for example, "difficulty enforcing his authority" (17, 18, 19) and that "man" "who is incap[able] of not ever wishing ~~ever~~ to go anwhere" and "is incap of living anywhere but at home" (12). Moore's repetition of "tomcat" is one of those instances where it is not clear whether she is playing with an idea not yet placed as part of a different poem ("Peter") or briefly imagining Adam as a tomcat (for "Marriage"). Moore also mentions "Bluebeard" (from "People's Surroundings") in relation to the line "I too am happy only at home" (11).

    Other of Moore's frequently repeated phrases include some variation on "not their silence but their silences" (11, 17)—shifting when Moore begins drafting specifically toward "Silence" (mid-page) to "not in silence but restraint" (92, 94, 97, 98, 99).[9] "Silence" comes closer to its published form than any other poem drafted in this notebook. Referring to Adam, Moore repeats variations on "I have seen him when he was so handsome he gave me a start" (19, 22, twice on 27, 39)—always among other lines pointing toward "Marriage." "An octopus of ice" first appears on page 6 and is then repeated three times several pages later (28, 66, 73). There are five references to a "goats looking glass" and another five to "Calypso the goats flower." Generally, around page 66 Moore turns from primary drafting of "Marriage" (first published 1923) toward primary drafting of "An Octopus" (published December 1924, shortly before its revised publication in *Observations*) and "Silence" (published October 1924).

While drafting toward "Marriage," Moore writes eight times a line she uses in the published poem: "men have power & sometimes one is made to feel it" (5, 14, 20, 22, 23, 25, twice on 27). She repeats other claims never appearing in the poem, for example, that marriage "is universally associated w the fear of loss" (8, 15, 19, 23, twice on 26 and 29, 50) and that "sentimental emancipation is a great aid to logic" (2, 7, 8, 20, 23, twice on 24, 28), once accompanied by the question "what are women emancipated fr & what are they being emancipated to?" (20). Later, Moore proposes that "the mind of man" (associated with "arrogance") "must be discarded . . . & forgetfulness be power. . . this eagle w tigers in his eyes & feet" (55). This passage occurs on a page beginning with "Marriage" centered, as a title, and then "the mud of matrimony"— trying out and cancelling a possible first line. If Moore did conceive of "Marriage" and "An Octopus" simultaneously, she seems soon to have made gender hierarchy exclusive to drafts of "Marriage"—although I find it difficult to place some references to "Adam" in one direction of drafting or the other. She repeats eleven times a variation on "eagle with tigers in its eyes and feet"—mostly in relation to descriptions of Adam; nothing in either poem makes use of this conception. She repeats five times some reference to the "spiked hand" that proves its affection "to the bone," perhaps a related portrayal.

The draft of a never published poem, apparently written in 1924, also picks up some of Moore's concerns with hierarchy and power, through a portrayal of animals.[10]

Unusually, this is an uninterrupted draft of one poem.

Vienna
~~A Cat~~   on Viennese striped silk
    a sleeping cat
    fanned by a rat
    an arctic fox on silk
    Venetian ~~fuschia—sultan red.~~
~~light blue and lilac silk.~~
             silver
  with 8 young rats in ~~scarlet~~ coats
to offer it, its milk—
    Venetian fuschia sultan red
    light blue & lilac silk
    Petunias here, petunias there,
    It has the only chair
and only pleased   Not wishing never to go anywhere
  at home   And happy only at home
                  a tyrant
  ~~It visits in its sleep~~   ~~surveying~~   in its sleep
  ~~the asiatic beast~~
Seets ~~Panama,~~ Niagra falls & Panama
~~& places in the east~~
It sits up taller than at first
  of conoisseurs of taste
    it is the smallest & the worst
       painting
[*Vertical left margin*: the raving ~~a decent~~ madman of good taste ~~It~~
~~is the~~ that eats when it is in the mood as much as any more
  than some it is the choicest & the worst]
[*Vertical right margin*: the silver cushioned chair]
  this ~~small horned~~ viper on a banner
    of blue & yellow silk
  as soft and snowy as that down
    adorns the blowballs frizzled crown—[11]

care ~~made w~~ care
the cushion,^ ~~settled there~~ [12]
by ~~monkeys~~ ~~art~~ hands—
Vienna bands ~~of~~
of silk on rabbit hair—
It has the only chair.

the morose mascot
    ideal companion for an indoor life

~~th~~ on cushion-cockle shells a pair
    ~~of~~ a pair of painted vipers on white silk
The innoucous child of fearless parents,
the tame cat—
the only domestic animal wh has not
        lost its wild quality

                        (*MMDA*, 07.04.04: 107-108)

Moore uses the phrases "the only domestic animal wh[ich] has not lost its wild quality" and "the innocuous child of fearless parents" in drafts toward "Silence" although not in the finished poem. "Peter" describes a cat with reference to its sleeping, to a chair, to an "eel" and "snake" (in "Vienna," the reference is to "vipers") and to his "disposition / invariably to affront" (*Becoming MM* 93, 94). This Viennese cat, however, is a "tyrant" and a "connoisseur" (perhaps the "worst"—a word Moore repeats): un-cat-like, it sits straight in "the only chair" and is fanned or fed by nine rats.

    In family nomenclature, Moore went by the nickname "Rat" from about 1914 for the rest of her life. Consequently, in some ways this poem suggests a portrait of Moore and her mother, Mary Warner Moore—with whom she was living in very cramped quarters. As Linda Leavell concludes in her biography *Holding on Upside Down*, this relationship both enabled Moore's writing career and was oppressive and troubling.[13] Her mother was, in some ways, tyrannical, and she did not like all of the poetry Moore was publishing. She may perhaps have been the "smallest and the worst" among "connoisseurs of taste" or "the choicest and the worst" among "madm[en] of good taste"—as "Vienna" puts it. Yet, the poem states, this "morose mascot" is the "ideal companion for an indoor life"—certainly true of an indoor cat, but perhaps also acknowledging that her life with Mary did enable her writing. Mary may also be "The innocuous child of fearless parents, / the tame cat" in that Moore and her brother referred to Mary as their child and themselves as her uncles.

This poem proposes a different kind of power relationship than a marriage, but perhaps one in which Moore similarly felt herself to be, or potentially to be, disadvantaged: as a woman in a marriage and as a "rat"/Rat in relationship to a tyrannical cat. Not much can be made of this poem since Moore abandoned it and its players are not distinctly developed. The cat is a "child" offered "milk" but also a tyrant fed by subject "rats." The phrase used earlier in relation to Bluebeard, "I too am happy only at home," now belongs to the cat ("it").[14] Neither cat nor rats are gendered and the scene is ekphrastic—describing a "banner" or "painting," or "cushion." Nonetheless, the poem repeatedly suggests relationships of power: the cat is a tyrant, a "viper," a raving madman, greedy (eating "more than some"—presumably more than others in its own household), monopolizing "the only chair," and alternately "morose," "innocuous," "tame," and "wild." Leavell's portrayal of Moore's eating disorder in relation to her mother's controlling behavior, especially in relation to food scarcity, encourages this interpretation of the drafted poem (Leavell 163-65).

As published, *Observations* is a remarkable volume. This 1920s poetry drafting notebook offers a fuller and still barely explored perspective on Moore's development and personal engagement with the topics and portrayals in the poems concluding that collection. Moreover, during the period between 1922, when she began keeping notebook 07.04.04, and the late 1924 publication of Observations, Moore was at least occasionally writing in six other reading, conversation, or miscellaneous-material notebooks. One of these, a reading notebook from 1923 (07.01.04), is also already published on the *MMDA*. As one of its editors, Claire Nashar, has written, this notebook's extensive index may provide a model for that of *Observations*.[15] Together the published poetry-drafting and reading notebooks; the not-yet-published five additional notebooks with material from 1922-1924; and the several reading, conversation, miscellaneous, and lecture notebooks she kept before 1922, offer new ways to consider the foreground and the accomplishment of *Observations*. It is my hope that this brief essay will encourage others to explore these and other notebooks for what they offer in relation to Moore's 1924 and later poems. And while such exploration may not alter evaluation of *Observations* per se, it cannot help but increase our understanding of Moore and the thinking that led to that extraordinary collection.

[1] Lawrence Buell, quoted *Leaves of Grass: The Sesquicentennial Essays*, eds. Susan Belasco, Ed Folsom, Kenneth Price. University of Nebraska Press, 2007, xiv.

[2] Gregory, *Apparitions of Splendor: Marianne Moore Performing Democracy through Celeberity*: 1952-1970. University of Delaware Press, 2021.

[3] All published poems are quoted from the 1924 *Observations* reprinted in facsimile in *Becoming Marianne Moore: The Early Poems 1907-1924*, edited Robin G. Schulze (University of California Press, 2002), abbreviated as *Becoming MM* (here page 90).

[4] Moore continues to draft in this notebook until 1930, including drafts of poems either published in the 1930s or never published.

[5] The Rosenbach Museum and Library refers to this notebook as VII.04.04. On the *MMDA* it is 07.04.04—to distinguish its published version from the Rosenbach MS, where the conserved pages have been bound in the wrong order. The *MMDA* edition restores the correct order to the notebook's pages. On the *MMDA*, the reference is to "images" (e.g., 0002); here, I refer to pages (e.g., 2). For this notebook, the two numbers are identical except for the "00"s. On the corrected order of pages, see Cristanne Miller, "A History of Moore Materials at the Rosenbach Museum & Library and the *MMDA*." *MMDA*, October 2018;

under "About: The Archive."

[6] Moore writes to Ezra Pound in 1919 that the form of her "original stanza" is "a matter of expediency" or chance, which she then repeats in other stanzas. *The Selected Letters of Marianne Moore*, eds Bonnie Costello with Celeste Goodridge and Cristanne Miller (Knopf, 1997): 122. Moore does not mention other aspects of her composition process. See *Margaret Holley, The Poetry of Marianne Moore: A Study in Voice and Value* (Cambridge University Press, 1987) on Moore's "model" stanza and for an excellent general discussion of her syllabic verse.

[7] See *Marianne Moore: Questions of Authority* (Harvard, 1995) Chapter 3 for my observations on Moore's use of "I" and general "Questions of Voice."

[8] Willis, "The Road to Paradise: First Notes on Marianne Moore's 'An Octopus.'" *Twentieth-Century Literature* 30.2-3 (1984): 242-266.

[9] The published poem contains the lines: "the deepest feeling always shows itself in silence; / not in silence, but restraint." All repeated phrases appear with some variation or abbreviation; I quote them in their most recognizable form.

[10] Moore does not date her drafts, but this draft occurs between phrases used in "Sea Unicorns and Land Unicorns" and so, logically, was written before that poem was published, in 1924.

[11] Moore indicates in her note on "Sea Unicorns and Land Unicorns" in *Observations*, the lines "As soft, and snowy, as that down / Adorns the Blow-ball's frizzled crown" comes from Charles Cotton's "An Epitaph on M.H." (*Becoming MM* 151).

[12] The caret (^) indicating textual insertion is mine.

[13] Leavell, *Holding on Upside Down: The Life and Work of Marianne Moore* (Farrar, Straus and Giroux, 2013).

[14] It is unclear whether the initial use of this phrase on page 2 reflects Moore's attitude or is quoted from her mother—who is mentioned, as "mole," in the line following "I too am happy only at home"; "mole" is family nomenclature for Mary Warner Moore. Other interpretations of its use on this page are possible, but these seem to me the most likely.

[15] Notebook 07.01.04, edited by Cristanne Miller and Claire Nashar; published *MMDA* 2022. See Nashar, "Marianne Moore and The Index." *Those Gendering Archives*. (The Center for Marginalia, Poetry Collection of the University at Buffalo, 2015). 8-12. Nashar is also working on a longer essay on Moore and indexing.

Dotty LeMieux

Birds, They Tell Us

Are not allowed in poetry anymore,
with their mouths full of fish, gullets
working overtime. Pelicans,
those acrobats of the air, oh so done
with them, they say. Give us
your open wounds, blood flowing.
Give us your heartache, cloaked in skin
fabric, poised on a knife's edge, not that
old trope of bird belly cut open
and stuffed full of plastic, or the one
where they cut the bill right off the pelican
and left it starving, unable
to call out.

Yeah, you cried. Get over it.

No metaphors but seams
of red running liquid, no truths
but sorrow from your glued tight mouth.
Your own dead child,
No birds. We've had it up to here
with red wing blackbirds
nightingales & swallows oh my god.

Especially the long legged
egret, most over-worked
of birds, mouth
full of flipping fish.
Hardest working bird

no longer dependent on poets'
handouts.

What of the turkey vulture, proud
on the gable, then
lifting off
helicopter like.
Velociraptor like,
in search of someone else's
lost prey, eagle-eyed
as an eagle
and twice as smart.

Birds, they tell us
all we need to know
if we listen
to their warbling song
hesitant and mocking all
at the same time.

I gather you my darlings, not
to kill you but to praise you.
My power line sitters,
my road-kill cleaners,
my stalk legged fish stabbers,
my warblers, impressionists,
raucous cawers, murmuring.

Murmuration makers.
Mockers, night flyers, hole drilling,
hippo cleaning,
crocodile flossing.
Useful ubiquitous
winged creatures.

I praise you, pray
to you, angels of
our daily life, even the cynical
poetry editor
on his bed of words, buried
in words,
cannot avoid
your insistent flapping and pecking
outside his shut tight window
made only of sand
and ash.

Taylor Franson-Thiel

In the Mingling Sounds of Ribbits and Rain

almighty tectonic plate I become, pulling
from my calf a key which unlocks the door
to the room containing the star I gave birth to.
I swallow it whole, unsettled at how sweet

it tastes to ignore my past. My name means to sew, to fix,
to stitch gossamer moondust to my eyelids
like I can pretend I don't remember the scent
of salt lakes or the trumpet call of marble temples.

Call it my personal atonement, as I look
at each planet and realize they are all mirrors.
I could skim pebbles across the surface of my
tongue, only to find they'll never sink.

I place a pointer finger in each ocean, then put both
to my tongue. Salt, more salt.

F.

Factis simul sideribus,
aetheris luminaribus,
collaudaverunt angeli
factura pro mirabili
immensae molis Dominum,
opificem caelestium,
praeconio laudabili,
desbito et immobili,
concentuque egregio
grates egerunt Domino
amore et arbitrio,
non naturae donario.

translated from Latin by Christian Lopac

Harmony of the Heavens

As soon as the stars
And their lights had been made,
The angels praised the Lord,
Who created through wonders
The immense, shapeless mass,
Fated and unmoving,
Praising with paeans
The Maker of the heavens.
They sing in a single harmony
Thanks to the Lord
Led not by nature's treasures
But love and choice.

I.

Invehunt nubes pontias
ex fontibus brumalias
tribus profundioribus
oceani dodrantibus
maris, caeli climatibus,
caeruleis turbinibus
profuturas segetibus,
vineis et germinibus,
agitatae flaminibus
thesauris emergentibus,
quique paludes marinas
evacuant reciprocas.

The Origin of the Sea

The clouds carry the sea
From its wintry origins—
The three deeper waters
Of the ocean's sea—
To the region of the sky.
Cerulean blue eddies
Nourish grains,
Vines, and shoots.
A blowing blast stirs
Treasures to rise
And empties the marsh
Back into the sea.

V.

Vagatur ex climactere
Orion caeli cardine
derelicto Virgilio
astorum splendidissimo;
per metas Thetis ignoti
orientalis circuli,
girans certis ambagibus
redit priscis reditibus,
oriens post biennium
Vesperugo in vesperum;
sumpta in problematibus
tropicis intellectibus.

The Celestial Christ

He moves from the highest point,
Orion, pivot of Heaven,
Leaving the Pleiades,
The greatest splendor,
Past the boundary of the unknown sea
Of the eastern belt.
Orbiting in fixed windings,
Having risen, the evening star returns
By ancient paths in the eveningtide.

Take these stars as riddles
With figurative meanings.

Esther Jansma

Te Lezen Bij Sneeuw

Een paar hoeken om en je staat in de stilte
op een bodem, tussen oude muren, lagen metselwerk
in zomaar een winter. Uit de tijd gestapt.

Het vriest. Kinderen - theemutsjes op lompe beentjes -
rapen takken en sneeuw van de grond net zoals zij
eeuwen geleden deden tussen de stenen

het gemetselde lapwerk in het zwijgen van het hof
waar als je goed luistert ijle stemmen misschien
de flarden van iets mateloos naar het heden zingen.

Dat is nu, vandaag. Het schemert al. De kinderen
spelen zoals ze spelen, omringd door tijd
waar jij niet bent. Jij kijkt naar hun herinneringen.

uit: 'Alles is nieuw', 2005

translated from Dutch by Arno Bohlmeijer

To be read when snow falls

Take a few corners and you're on a stone floor
in the silence, among old walls, layers of mortar
in simply a winter. Stepped out of time.

It's freezing. Children – tea-cosies on short blunt legs –
collect twigs and snow from the ground, just the way
it was done ages ago among the stones

the mortar patchwork in the silence of the court
where airy voices if you listen carefully may be singing
the fragments of 'measureless' toward the present.

That is now, today. It's twilight already. The children
are playing the way they play, surrounded by time
where you are not. It's their memories you watch.

Avishag Eliav

Fruit

He holds an orange
and looks at it intently
caressing with his thumb the textured exterior
"bumpy in all the right places"
he says with his eyes
piercing each pore
to the core he looks
but not for a heart or juicy fruit
he searches for a vessel beneath the skin
to open up violently and fill in.
He squeezes the orange
affectionately
the tips
of his fingers flash white for a brief moment
threatening to dig sharply into the young fruit
he is testing
whether the pulp has any give to it
what it can withstand
how far he can impose upon it
his desires
for fruit.

The orange begs
to peel it
but he does not
instead he turns her around in the palm of his hand
which is warm and smushy
but dry always
letting it feel his skin
letting it get hot from the slow gyral contact
minimizing friction
feigning generosity
subjecting the orange to his blank gaze.
The gaze that expertly veils truth
the gaze of pretend kindness
in the mouth, in the nose.
The gaze that is dead in the eyes
that looks for one thing only
"how can you be of use to me"
the dead eyes say
"you are an object"
and the orange pales
but does not wither;

My father's orange tree bore no fruit this season.
From my safe distance he informed me
"my tree bore no fruit this season";

For years we handled fruit.
And now I must eat alone
letting the vitamins of citrus
into my veins
to be of custom and of lore.
I peel slowly my orange
in my hand the enzymes and oils squirt
and leave cloudy strains on my palms
the color of cream soda.
When they dry
I get sticky and
irritable
trying to scratch off the marks
of impurity but in vain
for I only manage to wedge the smell of citrus deep under my nails
knowing damn well
every time I lift my hand to my face
for the next two days
I will smell it and I will remember;

I am sitting on my bed naked
wishing I were the orange
tonight
I do not eat this fruit;

When does it
all turn to juice?
When can I drink
refreshments?
My skin dries beneath the wet gaze
and dampens when dead eyes look upon it,
searches to be whole
and torn and wholed again
by some father's child.
Squished to juice between two metal spheres
that cut perfectly into the halved orange
droplets dribble through the small holes
collecting in a cup centimeters below
that feel like eons of space.
He looks at me directly
as he drinks to satiety
his eyes completely
and utterly
dead;

James Ph. Kotsybar

The There There

Able to blend the oils of Matisse with the vinegar of Picasso
Gertrude Stein was like some leafy-green of the art world,
from her salad days on, but she was no Iceberg
nor, *let us* say, bland.
Maybe she was more of an artichoke.

While ghost-written Toklas played the hostess,
Stein was "*Subject With Intrinsic Background,*"
who blurred the lines of relational importance,
and allowed all of the art
and all the arts to mix, harmoniously or not.

Though the imp in her could offend even Hemingway
with one word, the color of banana,
he was still more ape for her in admiration
than his gorilla machismo could ever admit.

If not for her,
drunken Joyce might have thrown "Moore" of Magritte's apples at Duchamp,
while aloof Man Ray   just clicked pictures
at quite nearly   metronomic pace,
but Stein quickly stepped in to
cube up the rest to send home
with Cézanne from the Salon,
before things got "Wilder."

This regular nexus
of cultivated creativity
that arose
was the rose

(I propose)
in Gertrude's garden, lush with achievements

(and probably artichokes).

Abhishek Udaykumar
Middle World

Scarves of wind

heave the plains

till they are deserted

in cacti fields –

Past tins of diners and bagels scabbed with maps of cargo trains.
Through cigars of chimneys wrapped with dehydrated rain and the
weight of people's affairs.

leeks of hay

and bottlebrush birds

find refuge

on skeletal billboards –

A single string guitar shivers through the sleepy sawdust, for muted
secrets buried beneath coir beds. As opal eyed teens in blue overalls
walk to cavernous schools.

making bets

over teenage things

as lovers scuffle

against lovers –

Breaths of brandy licking pool clubs swig the sand dunes to *Paris, Texas*
tunes. Broke and alone, lipstick loners hang out in hopes of beery love
and the iron rain.

Margaret Marcum
Are women sponges

or lamps with curved lights or
glimmering stickers on fast cars,
impermanent and alive with desire for
more speed, more road ahead, always
more sights where I feel different

You might be driving faster, but I'm using
my time just to have fun

Hot pink pouted lips on top of the
Christmas tree, I wanted action figures
not heroes, but we watched the small train
from so far away it looked like just a line

Holes in the bottom of my shoes,
that's where my money should be,
holes in the wall,
that's where my eyes should be,
holes in my soul,
that's where you should be

Candy

Sour patch kids you
are my favorite place I
taste the sweet nectar from
the same gods you drink
from when I am happy.

When we're apart so
is my mother from her child,
her tears are so loud I can't
dream at night—the illusion of you
and her are all that fill my room,
and I can't sleep here anymore though
I know it's only temporary.

Mazzy Sleep
Too Far In

Planted in the heart of the question,
Tendrils whipping out like flames—
Why raise a child to be feral
When you're already tamed?

Question marks are wounds pressed deeper
Incantations summoning nothing,
Or maybe a chiming thought
If you're lucky, if it works, the paper goes unpaved

A hand without fingers or a palm,
The unearthliness, the vulnerability of wrists
A look-what-you-made-me-do ilk of bitterness
There's a difference between going with the flow
And taking the hits

You poise yourself like a livelihood
That those veils are for stamped beauty,
Not the skittering reality that you need a hiding place—
Dashing away the moment you learn life isn't a race

Only so much you can put in one poem,
An agglomeration of reasonings, of causes
That one hopes lack consequence
What did we do it for? When, why, how?

History needs more structure,
Why go in chronological order
When you have the alphabet?

Why put you before me
When I am the one writing?

If you build the world off a stack of
Assumptions, does the originality vanish
Under rounds of alter(c)ations and changes,
Or is it there forever, waiting for its return?

Are we stuck in an infinite state
Are we too young or are we too late

dust cover shell

dust cover shell
    take cover!
yank my arm & shiver with delight; be my light?
shine so bright
it hurts
    if everyone here was asked
    to choose between me and
    you, they'd choose me
wipe a tear
live in fear
memories under the bed
broken doorframe where i hit my head
    sky blue sky blue
    everyone is out except for y-o-u—
hearts on a page
lazy love you
dove with twisted wing
flower that blooms underwater

a delicate rose
naturally unnatural pose

1964
oil on canvas

Yolanda Hansen

I'm sorry I was late

For Fern

I'm sorry I was late, I was distracted
by a muskrat. I had every intention of coming
to your workshop, pen and notebook
ready, but I took a walk and chanced
upon a muskrat in the back
pond, a sleek wet triangle
pulling a fresh-chewed bundle of reeds
in its mouth, longer than its submerged body
in the algae-spotted calm, and was arrested,
I had to get closer,
so I stumbled down the weed strewn ditch
heedless of ticks, to crouch, breath lodged
in my throat like a stone, to watch this V
of reeds and fur beeline through the meandering
ruddy ducks, straight to me and all my frozen limbs,
and the redwing blackbirds were singing
and the frogs were croaking and oh,
I knew I was late, but I couldn't tear
myself away, the breeze a gift
on my face and I thought *this is gratitude*,
and I couldn't bear
to be inside
four closed walls again.

Grasslands National Park in 50,000 Blinks

If humans blink 20 times a minute, let me
stretch
                    my wonder by hours so I can look upon the
                        vastness
                                of grass anchoring the world. I struggle
                                to pin down
                                            my awe,   fail.

                            An ocean of stems,
                    infinity of leaf blades and sheaths,
                unending plate of grass under a bowl of sky.

            Spear grass,
            wheat grass,
            blue gramma.

        Blink once,
        twice
        a hundred times,
        the bend and sway
        are not the same.

I stretch my eyelids to   catch
the corners of my vision but I can't grasp
its edges. There are no
trees to bracket my sight.
The horizon orbits me
                like a moon.

When I did become so small?

                    I am
                    an ant,
                            a fly speck,
                            the blink of an eye.

Tjizembua Tjikuzu

To the Master of Silence

I sense you rise
in me—
your tongue inflamed,
reddened,
and bloated with speech.

I feel your shadow
at the margins of my dreams,
hovering over my body
like a farmer inspecting
the ripeness of his fruits.

You are a thief
at 3:00 a.m. stumbling over
the fence
of my dream world
as if burdened
by a sack of secrets.

When you crawl
past the fence, your back
is a formidable wall
against my song.

You refuse to look
at my face—
Will your tongue explode?
Will our dream burn
to smithereens if you speak?

When you unmask,
your eyes
are always on the floor,
swathed in shadows
like a wounded cat.

But tonight, I have left
all the lights
of my dream world on:
I am dusting every square inch
of space and time;
I am shining a bright flash
light in your fermented silence;
I am rattling the walls
of my dreams
like a sangoma
beguiling the feline
and bird bones
to augur good fortune;

I have become a bat
hurtling through the night,
spinning the silvery strings
of echo into music.

June Bugs

In January we sail kites that feast
on the camel thorn bush breaking
in bloom outside our grandparents' yard.
After sour milk and pap,
my brothers and I raid the bush:
yanking out dark-green June bugs with bold cream lines
bordering their exoskeleton shell; or leaf green
with white spots on their abdomen; or dull brown
with broad shells and strong joints; or rare light brown
with tiny black spots from thorax to elytra.
We find them grinding the bush's branches,
bleeding out the stems with their diligent mandibles.
We pluck one each from the nest,
clasp it in our small hands, the serrations
on their legs grazing against our sweaty palms
as they lumber to crawl out—
their tiny compound eyes and antennae
cowering under the soft taut flesh of palm.
Using our grandmother's knitting thread, snatched
from her 1936 Singer Sewing Machine,
we take the long thread at its end and make a knot
with a hole wide enough for a June bug's hind leg,
then tie two or three knots,
tethering the kite, so it wouldn't escape.
We like the bulky, dull brown
with strong joints best; their legs never separate
from their abdomen, even when we yank the line.
We fly them for hours—their wings
droning hard to reach the unreachable.
Giving them the thread, the false freedom,
then taking away the thread's length again,

holding them at arm's length,
to hear better, the music of their labor.
Our faces beam with delight:
eyes squinting to avoid the Kalahari sun,
nostrils flaring as we work the thread,
mouths curling in everlasting giggles
as if we are watching a funny puppet show.
At the end of playtime, we feed the dead
to chickens and sands, free those
that can still fly, and return the broken
legged, broken winged back to the nest
for more sugar and water—
our hands bug-shit-stained and loud with sap.

Wendeline

The Red purse.
      Red worn-out leather
      purse. Golden eagle dollar
in withered hands.

I cannot place your face
exactly.

Lady of toenails twisted like
the horns of a mountain goat;

I have your marks in me.

Your voice? All
gone now, muffled, like dry leaves
buried in the fatty flunk
of a sleeping puff adder.

In the chaotic mornings
of our kicks and wails,
your walking club is the sting
of a desert scorpion
on our clean-shaven heads.

Red purse
in brown weathered hands.
Your golden dollar feeds me.
Feeds me like bread.
More than bread.

Grandmother, red lady.
Red lady of warring bloods.

It is you I come for courage in the dark.

You lady of heavy winds and spirits.
You lady of fermented peas and hymns.

When the mountains close in,
I whisper your forbidden name
in the hungry wind:
Kauniva, Kauniva, Kauniva.
And the night parts in threes.

CLS Sandoval

Surreal Evening

The dog arched like a Halloween cat
There was black and white static on a streaming app
The cookie dough ice cream had nuts in it
The kernels wouldn't pop on the stove or in the microwave
The sound of the wind was louder that the cat's hiss
The plants seemed taller than during the day
The clock displayed a time that didn't seem to match the mood

Elaine Verdill
Dinosaur Pond

These winter hens
  Come cluck to the waterhole
Flutter their feather dust all the way
Too invalid to lay their eggs
      Their old walnut-brains just keep on glaring

 Proud direct descendants of T. Rex
              Or his cousins' stone bones

        Eggs from the old landscape

When the dustbowls were mighty tar pits of dare
These winter hens
     Cluck around the nested ponds
Migrate west to east, walkabout

Fluffed to the winds and spring traditions
    Daffodil chicks
  Brighten this old farm

Campaign Cat

as the cat domesticated
      the feral canine, he
explained
        there is no translation of dog into
           the feline world view

and then they got along fine

        now I tell the cat
it's impossible for him
      to run for city council
          just to see what he will do

Samantha Malay

Equinox

this morning I put clean sheets on the bed
and remembered it was still summer last week

I didn't pick blackberries
or wade in the lake
like I said I would

but I rationed a bag of plums
from my brother's tree
buried a bird I found on the park path
watched the sun move across the kitchen wall
as I washed dishes
on my days off

Reginald Saint-Vincent Paul
Mirror-Mirror

A top star Dog
pets, pat, rail, stab
regal diva model's
evil mined stun buns.

No spit tool tips emit
sleek dew on deer skin.
But seldom repaid
stressed loots, meets
a mad rat's stool.

Stop, live, wolf & level:
Trot sod yard.
Span stink-eye!
Tap bad desserts.
Wed straw dam.

Top's taps flow draw
sleep, noon naps, ward room.
Racecar, Dray, Kayak…
Reviver(s) defied!

I am, Moor, saw Madam God
civic radar maps, redder!
Refer Eve repay liar peels way
was swap, no-parts w/ reel
strap-on keel boy-pit!

Redivider… leer!
Sway not.
I got avid do's
paws, nuts, time.

Nina Knueven
homeostasis

You pull off dead rose heads
and you sprinkle more plant food
                  And wait for new buds
You love friend one
                  And you love friend two
            But they say awful things of each other
Once to discipline your time
You committed with your mouth
                  Then planted your feet lifeless
Sometimes you even believe yourself
                  When arguing about rain with others
It's not that you want to have written the book
                  But to lift the lining of each page
And rearrange the letters into the right order
                  You want your words to be of the page
You don't want an ending
              That is sad of its hopeful beginning
      You want a real impersonator
      one who knows what dirt feels like

poem without gravity

Instead, the poem is weightless & floating

Not quite flight
            but hovering above without
        rigid corseting back to earth

This might be true nature—no stiff joints from weight bearing

  no compacted vertebrae
                        no real deadlines   low crime

Poems float
along as they please:
        the body immaterializes
        No forced social interactions or fear of falling intrude the poem

            Drifting above
        the ocean is simple

                quiet & isolating like a singular ball of mercury singing

                without glass

Since the poem is no longer compressed
it can raise its arms to the stars in blank trajectory

                        but it doesn't cascade towards them either

                    The poem lacks the need for meaning

like spring pollen that doesn't land anywhere

The poem doesn't endure analytical conversation

for no poems remains close enough to one another

The poem must secure itself down to maintain control

Although there is no coerced cling to earth, there is still inertia

The poem becomes obsessed with changing
& creates its own force

It pulls to push off objects & people & other poems

We don't know where the poem will land

But its mass craves other masses

B.A. Van Sise

Vesuvio

Sono stato, ultimamente,
ossessionato dalle cose.
Ultimamente significa tutta la mia vita.
Ultimamente significa un diapason
vibrato contro un tavolo,
una cosa solida urtata
contro un'altra cosa solida
per diventare liquida nell'aria.
Per *cose* intendo l'odore
dei forni a legna.
Per *cose* intendo il suono
dei rondoni fuori dal
grigio appartamento dove,
sì, vivo ancora, nonostante
non dedichi altro che il pensiero a
una vita migliore. Per *forni*
intendo casa. Per *rondoni*
intendo te. Certe mattine
non riesco a respirare quando provo
a immaginare come potrei mai,
forse, vivere senza di te,
anche se lo faccio da anni.

Vesuvius

I have been, lately,
obsessing about things.
By *lately* I mean all my life.
By *lately* I mean a tuning fork
twanged against a table,
one solid thing thumped
against another solid thing
to then look liquid in the air.
By *things* I mean the smell
of wood burning ovens.
By *things* I mean the sound
of sparrows outside the
gray apartment where, yes,
I still live, despite giving
nothing but thought to a
better life. By *ovens* I
mean home. By *sparrows*
I mean you. Some mornings
I can't breathe when I try
to imagine how I could ever,
possibly, live without you,
even though I've been
doing it for years.

Luke Carson

Observations' Index

Inaccessible for many years outside of the 1924 and then the corrected 1925 edition of *Observations*, Marianne Moore's idiosyncratic index to her first book (leaving out the 1921 *Poems* published without her authorization) is now readily available in three editions of her work: Robin Schulze's 2002 facsimile edition of Moore's early work, including *Observations*; Linda Leavell's 2016 edition of *Observations*; and Heather White's 2017 edition of *New Collected Poems*. Readers who had never seen the original may have been familiar with the convenient index (organized alphabetically by title and first line) to the long-standard Moore text, the Penguin *Collected Poems* – still regrettably available in any used bookstore – would be sure to notice more of an authorial than editorial hand in its composition. There is no comment on the index that I am aware of in the original reviews of Moore's work, perhaps because readers were engaged enough and likely overwhelmed by the intricate arrays of detail in the poems; or perhaps a glance at the index reassured some readers that someone – an editor? the author? – had perceived a sense of order and provided a thematic and topical guide.

We can be sure that Louis Zukofsky noticed and kept it in mind as he composed the delightful "Index to Names and Objects" to *A*, the long poem that he started in 1928 and completed in 1974. Nonetheless, while Moore's "Notes" drew critical attention, the "Index" went unremarked, and it has continued that way, apart from some passing observations and more recently an enjoyable article by Rebecca Bradburn in a scholarly journal called *The Indexer*, which reassured me that I was not wrong to think that readers and reviewers remained silent on the matter. Nor does anything in Moore's published letters provide any sense of her decision to include an index or the process of building it. There is one hint of her interest in the possibility in a 1921 letter in which she thanks Bryher for an "exquisite" book of the poems of Henri de Régnier, the French Symbolist poet, "with its flowered cover, sheafs of wheat and remarkable little index." The editors of the letters suggest that the book is probably de Régnier's 1921 *Vestigia flammae*, but the likelihood is higher that it is the 1921 edition (the twentieth!) of his 1900 book *Les Médailles d'Argile*, which opens with the much-discussed (by Amy Lowell in 1915 and others) poem "J'ai feint que des Dieux m'aient parlé" that René Taupin revealed in 1929 had been an influence on Ezra Pound's "The Return."

The imagery that Moore goes on to describe in the letter corresponds not only to imagery in the poem and other poems in the book but also to the caduceus with serpents printed on its title page. However, at 252 pages and roughly 5" by 7", can this be the "tiny" book Moore describes? And is its unremarkable table of contents, placed at the back of the book as is standard for French publications, anything like "a remarkable index"? It seems fitting to me that it is seemingly impossible to trace Moore's reference back to an object: I feel that this has to be the book she is talking about, but also that it cannot be this book. And in my wishfulness I think there must a book of poems, lost in an archive somewhere, and apparently not at the Rosenbach Museum and Library, that contains "the remarkable" – perhaps Borgesian – "index" that inspired Moore to create her own extraordinary index that so manifestly, because of its largely unknown principles of inclusion, cannot be intended simply for use.

Some hopeful readers, though they were clearly reduced to silence along with their contemporaries, may have sought to detect in the index a hint of a poet's arcane symbolism ("Hermes," "Merlin," the hieroglyphic "ibis," the symbolic "chrysalis" or the symbolist "Swans," although with the latter the plural and capitalized noun misrepresents the one "swan" it points to on page 35). Later and more experienced readers of Moore might think to see the projection of an imaginative universe of recurrent words and images (for example, "Swans" looks forward to "No Swan So Fine" and the two entries for "bat" look forward to the bat of "Nine Nectarines and Other Porcelain"; even the "beau with the muff" – on which more below – may look forward to the "grandmother's muff" of "Half-Deity"). At times, though rarely, there is metaphorical or thematic emphasis, as when two different appearances of "collision" – "of knowledge" and "of orchids" – get one entry. (Then "orchids, collision of" gets a separate entry while "knowledge" has an entry unrelated to "collision.") One clear principle is that all the titles of the poems will appear (though I have not confirmed it); another is that most of the titles will appear several times in redundant variation.

My sometime favorite is "HE WROTE THE HISTORY BOOK," which reappears one entry later as "HISTORY BOOK, see HE," with its emphatic masculine pronoun. Then why is "FOOL, A, A FOUL THING, A DISTRESSFUL LUNATIC" not followed almost immediately by "FOUL THING, see FOOL," since we can also find the title under "DISTRESSFUL LUNATIC, see FOOL" and "LUNATIC, see FOOL"? (Right above "LUNATIC" is the Thoreauvian or Coleridgean "loon.") I would find that redundancy satisfying, though my desire is unreasonable and the index as it is surely suffices, though I don't doubt it could have assumed innumerable other forms. Quietly drawing attention to the process of indexing is the title "PICKING AND CHOOSING," which appears first as "CHOOSING, PICKING AND," which invites us to consider other procedures of desiring selection, emphasizing also that to choose and to pick are not synonymous and other overlapping concepts, like opting, are to be considered; and looking back at the title we could begin to think that there is more opposition between PICKING and CHOOSING than there is synonymy: a more nuanced sense of CHOOSING may imply moral profundity (see "*feeling* 55, 97," 113) and the challenge of finitude than PICKING does, which could follow more playful and less risk-fraught procedures (choosing one over another versus picking one of many). "FEAR IS HOPE" is uttered in a different rhetorical register when the syntax is inverted in "HOPE, FEAR IS," one of a few phrases in the index that is a grammatical statement (other examples are "I envy nobody" under "Compleat Angler" and "envy nobody," an imperative that gets its own entry). Poem titles that begin with "IN" or "TO" are listed at least twice, once with and once without the preposition (and then of course they are further subdivided by nouns).

This division and recombination of phrases happens only once among the non-titular entries, and it is one of my favorite redundancies: "Adventures in Bolivia" reappears as "Bolivia, Adventures in," referring to a 1922 book – one certainly not known to many of Moore's contemporaneous readers – by C. H. Prodgers, whose name is also indexed. These are among the many hyperspecific references one can't imagine anyone looking up, such as "four o'clock, 78" – another favorite – and "pulled, 20," unless the purpose of the index were to remind you of every stray detail (which it isn't because it doesn't and the index does not fail in achieving its unidentified purpose). But the idiosyncratic and hyperspecific items – "learned scenery, 72" – are side-by-side with generic ones, like "bears," and those in between the specific and the generic, like "chipmunk, nine-striped" and "bear, tailed" – misalphabetized to come after the hyperspecific "beau with muff." Though when we look to the poem with the tailed bear it is actually "the long-tailed bear," certainly more specific than the tailed bear, since all bears have at least a vestigial tail, or at least a tailless bear must be more rare than a tailed one, which is perhaps why Moore implicitly corrects Prodgers in her poem (for which see UNICORNS, SEA, or SEA UNICORNS AND LAND UNICORNS but not UNICORNS, LAND or LAND UNICORNS or you will not find it). According to Prodgers, who cites Rowland Ward, who also appears in the index though not every name does, the tailed bear is only found in Ecuador – which gets its own entry as "Ecquador" in the uncorrected 1924 index. But why would it not be entered as "bear, tame and concessive"? Could not the two entries involving beavers just below the bears have been combined into the one common term, "beaver"? No, because one principle is that singular and plural nouns get separate entries (cf. "butterfly," "butterflies," and "orchid," "orchids"; but also cf. "Swans" for one swan) I am happy they weren't, since I do like to read "beavers, thoughtful," and their thoughtfulness would appear to be a precondition of them being "beavers making drains," which for a moment I can think is what Rimbaud's beavers were building after the flood.

Sometimes the index includes and excludes simultaneously: "Blake, W., 96" leaves out his appearance on page 98. In the end, exclusion reigns, however, and not only because some of Moore's sources in the notes are left blank – as in the "someone writes of" on page 98 – and therefore not indexed ("the queen full of jewels," the counterpart of "the beau with the muff," is included in a note on page 99 but the source is left blank and this queen, who readers eventually learned from Patricia Willis is Queen Anne, is, like the source, excluded from the index; but sometimes the blanks seem conscientiously to mean "Ibid.," as with the one following the note on W. R. Gordon on page 102). I'm quite sure that none of the people or places in the Whitmanian list of "People's Surroundings" appears in the index, though that capacious poem has over 30 items indexed, including "pugs," "dromios," and "Utah." There is a giddy delight in the process of picking and choosing, including and excluding. Like a poem, it engages interest and desire; once set in motion by reading, the circulation of words and phrases is dizzyingly expansive and contractive. If you read long enough in Moore's work, I think, every experience of a formal principle in operation is given a name, and the index substantiates the notion of "conscientuous inconsistency."

CONTRIBUTORS

CONTRIBUTORS

GLEN ARMSTRONG (he/him) holds an MFA in English from the University of Massachusetts, Amherst and edits a poetry journal called *Cruel Garters*. His poems have appeared in *Conduit*, *Poetry Northwest*, and *Another Chicago Magazine*.

REMON BADAN is a Christian Palestinian poet from the city of Nazareth, Israel. He is a 2nd year student at Tel Aviv University (English Literature MA). Back in 2022, he won first place in the Bessin 2023 Poetry Competition.

AKHMET BAITURSYNULY (1872-1937) was a highly influential Kazakh intellectual both creatively and politically. Not only a leading member of the Kazakh nationalist group Alash Orda, Baitursynuly also adapted the Arabic script to be used with the Kazakh language. After his execution in 1937, his work in politics, education, poetry, and linguistics were mostly forgotten. A victim of the Great Purge, his memory has since been rehabilitated and he is appreciated as one of the intellectual forefathers of modern Kazakhstan. These poems come from his distinctly political and most well-known collection *Masa* ("*Mosquito*"). They have never before been translated to the English language.

ESENIA BANUELOS is a living Mexican-American word-wreath from Chicago, Illinois. She is an undergraduate double-major in Educational Studies and Linguistic & Language in the Quaker Consortium and a preschool aide for the Phebe Anna Thorne School in Bryn Mawr, Pennsylvania. Her work is rooted in the semantic and syntactic revolution of Chicano identity and confronting the generational traumas of NAFTA, Bracero, and mixed status living.

YONATAN BERG is a contemporary Hebrew language poet and the youngest recipient of the Yehuda Amichai Prize and a number of other national awards. He has published three books of poetry, one memoir and two novels. *Frayed Light*, his first poetry collection in English, published by Wesleyan Press, was a finalist in The Jewish Book Awards. Berg is a bibliotherapist and teaches creative writing in Jerusalem. His poems in English translation by Joanna Chen have been published in *Consequence, Moment Magazine, Lunch Ticket, Poetry International* and *World Literature Today*, among others.

A. J. BERMUDEZ is an award-winning writer and filmmaker who currently serves as Editor of *The Maine Review* and Visiting Assistant Professor of Creative Writing at the University of Miami. Her work has been featured at the Yale Center for British Art, Sundance, the LGBT Toronto Film Festival, and in a number of literary publications, including *The Kenyon Review, Virginia Quarterly Review, Chicago Quarterly Review, Boulevard, Story*, and elsewhere. She is a former boxer and EMT, a current Steinbeck Fellow and Lambda Award Finalist, and is a winner of the Pushcart Prize, the Diverse Voices Award, the Page Award, the Alpine Fellowship Writing Prize, and the Iowa Short Fiction Award.

AVIVA BETZER writes in both English and Hebrew. She majored with honors in the studies of Theory of Literature at Tel Aviv University and wrote her thesis on the representations of the Freudian body in the fiction of David Vogel. Her work has been published in *Caesura, Chambers Anthology, Arc, The Foundationalist* and her published book of poetry in Hebrew, *Noise*. Another publication is forthcoming in Voices. She is currently a graduate student in the Department of English Literature and American Studies at Tel Aviv University.

ARNO BOHLMEIJER is a novelist, poet, and translator, writing in English and Dutch, winner of a PEN America Grant 2021, published in six countries, two dozen renowned journals and reviews, and in *Universal Oneness: An Anthology of Magnum Opus Poems from around the World*, 2019. His novel *SHELTERING* will appear in 2024. www.arnobohlmeijer.com

S. T. BRANT lives in Las Vegas where he teaches high school English and Journalism. His debut collection *Melody in Exile* was published in 2022. His work has appeared and is forthcoming in numerous journals including *Honest Ulsterman, EcoTheo, Timber, Rain Taxi, Ocean State Review, Green Mountains Review, Ekstasis*, and *New South*. He is the founder of the online reading series In the Fire Garden that hosts virtual readings and interviews with emerging and established writers. He can be contacted through his website at ShaneBrant.com, Twitter: @terriblebinth, or Instagram: @shanelemagne

LAWRENCE BRIDGES' poetry has appeared in *The New Yorker*, *Poetry*, and *The Tampa Review*. He has published three volumes of poetry: *Horses on Drums* (Red Hen Press, 2006), *Flip Days* (Red Hen Press, 2009), and *Brownwood* (Tupelo Press, 2016). You can find him on IG: @larrybridges

EDWARD BURKE, under the anonym "strannikov", has written flash fiction (absurdism, science satire, noir humor) and essays since 2011 appearing in various online venues. His verse (since 2016) has appeared online at *Fictionaut*, *Literati Magazine*, *Dead Mule School of Southern Literature*, *Oddball Magazine*, and in print at *Chiron Review*.

LUKE CARSON teaches modern and contemporary American poetry at the University of Victoria in British Columbia. He has written and co-written several articles on Moore, among other poets. He is an Associate Director of the editorial board of the *Marianne Moore Digital Archive* and the Series Editor for the datebooks of Marianne Moore.

N.T. CHAMBERS writes about the emotions and experiences intrinsic to human nature. Numerous works have been published in the following magazines: *Grassroots*, *The Banyan Review*, *Inlandia*, *The Orchard Poetry Journal*, *The Decadent Review*, *Quibble Magazine*, *Red Coyote*, *Bluebird Word*, *Bookends Review*, *Blaze Vox*, *Black Coffee Review*, *In Parentheses* and *SBLAAM*.

JOANNA CHEN is a writer and literary translator whose full-length literary translations include Agi Mishol's *Less Like a Dove* (Shearsman Books, 2016), Yonatan Berg's *Frayed Light* (Wesleyan Poetry Series, 2019; and Meir Shalev's *My Wild Garden* (Penguin Random House, 2020), among others. Chen's translation of Tehila Hakimi's "Hunting in America" won the 2023 Paper Brigade Award for Israeli Fiction. She teaches literary translation at the Helicon School of Poetry and contributes to *The Los Angeles Review of Books*.

Born in 1993, CHEN POYU has won numerous literary prizes in Taiwan, including the Lin Rong San Poetry Award and China Times Literary Award. He is the author of *The Bubbles Maker* (essays), and two poetry collections, *mini me*, and recently, *The Art of Rivalry*. His Chinese translation of Robert Hass' *Summer Snow* was published in 2022. He currently lives in Taipei. IG: @lukepoyudchen

MARIA DA CUNHA (October 19, 1872-January 10, 1917) was born in Lisbon to a well-to-family to a Brazilian mother and Spanish father. da Cunha was a poet and journalist. Her first book of poems was released in 1909, the preface written by Júlio Dantas boosted sales. A new edition with added poems was released in 1911. Her second volume, *O Livro da Noite* was released in 1915. Her lover, Virgínia Quaresma, was one of the first Portuguese people to be openly gay. There's some speculation that their move to Brazil, Cunha had a teaching job and Quaresma to write for a periodical, was influenced by a desire for anonymity and to escape a homophobic environment. Cunha's sudden death saw Quaresma return to Portugal and a bright talent gone too soon.

When GUY D'ANNOLFO (M.A.) isn't battling impostor syndrome at his day job, or kindling a love of Natural History with his son, or accidentally disrupting the peace in a Satipaṭṭhāna class, he's likely to be found doing what he loves most: writing and reading poetry. Guy's poems have been published by the *Schuylkill Valley Journal*, *The Courtship of Winds*, *Paperbark*, *Chestnut Review*, and *Cape Cod Times*.

EUGENE DATTA is the author of the poetry collection *Water & Wave* (Redhawk, 2024). His recent work has appeared or is forthcoming in *The Dalhousie Review*, *Main Street Rag*, *Common Ground Review*, *Amarillo Bay*, *Hamilton Stone Review*, and elsewhere. He has received fellowships or residencies from Stiftung Laurenz-Haus, Ledig House International Writers' Colony, and Fundación Valparaíso. Born in India, he lives in Aachen, Germany.

LAINE DERR holds an MFA from Northern Arizona University and has published interviews with Carl Phillips, Ross Gay, Ted Kooser, and Robert Pinsky. Recent work has appeared or is forthcoming from *J Journal*, *Full Bleed* + The Phillips Collection, *ZYZZYVA*, *Portland Review*, *Prairie Schooner*, and elsewhere.

THOM EICHELBERGER-YOUNG (T E-Y) is an artist and mental health caregiver raised in the Carolinas and now living in Missouri. Their art explores issues of poetics, gender, perception, war, and violence through research and documentary practices. In 2021, they founded Blue Bag Press, which focuses on chapbooks by innovative writers, and they will begin a PhD in Poetics this fall at SUNY Buffalo. Their first book is *BESPOKE* (published by Saint

Andrews in 2019). New work is available in the catalog to Blowing Rock Art & History Museum's *Ars Poetica* exhibit, *In Parentheses*, as well as Belladonna* Collaborative's *Germinations*, and forthcoming in *Magazine1*, *Antiphony*, *Canary* and *Bombay Gin*.

KURT COLE EIDSVIG is the author of *OxyContin for Breakfast*, *Art Official*, and *Pop X Poetry*.

AVISHAG ELIAV is an undergraduate student at Tel Aviv University, pursuing a double major in Geography and English Literature. Reading and writing from a young age, she enjoys novels and contemporary poetry. Avishag hopes to pursue a career in urban planning while still making time to frequent the beach and write.

SOPHIE EWH is a writer, filmmaker, and educator practicing radical openness in her art. When they discovered Whose Line is it Anyway?, she learned how to laugh. After developing an obsession with B-horror movies and mental breakdowns, she tried to make others laugh but mostly just made them nauseous. They are the editor of 1.5 Million, a documentary about literacy in The Bronx, and a graduate of NYU's Creative Writing MFA in poetry. You can find their writing in *The Poetry Society of New York*, *Through Lines Magazine*, and *Munster Literature*, among others.

KRIS FALCON's second poetry collection was recently published. Her latest publications appear in *The Lake*, *Pinhole Poetry*, *Anti-Heroin Chic*, and elsewhere. She has been nominated for a Pushcart Prize. She received her MFA at the School of the Art Institute of Chicago.

ROBERT FERNANDEZ is the author of *Scarecrow* (Wesleyan University Press, 2016), as well as *Pink Reef* (2013) and *We Are Pharaoh* (2011), both published by Canarium Books. He is also cotranslator of *Azure* (Wesleyan University Press, 2015), a translation of the work of Stéphane Mallarmé. www.robert-fernandez.com

ELEONORA FOGLIA holds a classical studies degree, is currently an international jurisprudence student at the University of Naples, and is the poet, B.A. Van Sise's long-suffering niece.

TAYLOR FRANSON-THIEL is a poet from Utah, now based in Fairfax, Virginia. She received her Master's in creative writing from

Utah State University and is pursuing an MFA at George Mason University. Her writing frequently centers on the intersections between the female body, religion, and her experiences as a college athlete. You can find her work in places such as *Psaltery and Lyre*, *Quarter Press*, *The Bangalore Review* and others. Along with writing, she enjoys lifting heavy weights and reading fantastic books.

STEVE GERSON, Emeritus English Professor, writes poetry and flash about life's dissonance. He has published in *CafeLit*, *Panoplyzine*, *Crack the Spine*, *Decadent Review*, *Vermilion*, *In Parentheses*, *Wingless Dreamer*, *Big Bend Literary Magazine*, *Coffin Bell*, and more, plus his chapbooks *Once Planed Straight*; *Viral*; *And the Land Dreams Darkly*; and *The 13th Floor: Step into Anxiety* from Spartan Press.

J. S. GRAHAM is an emerging poet from Yorktown, Virginia. His research interests include critical policy analysis, secondary specialty centers, and distance education. He writes for the friends he's made along the way.

Monk poet GUAN-XIU (832-912) was a renowned Chan (Zen) Buddhist hermit, wanderer, and artist of many disciplines at a turmoil time of Medieval China. Like many Chan monks before him, he embodied poetry in his religious meditation and vice versa. Unlike those hermits of peaceful times, he wandered the war torn landscape in the aftermath of one of the most tragic periods in Chinese and human history. Reflecting this drastic social change, he was one of the first to break through the old poetic conventions, as we see him experiment with more vernacular tones, more humanistic perspectives, and more variable musical patterns.

DINÇER GÜÇYETER grew up as the son of a barkeeper and blue-collar worker. He went to night school to finish his high school diploma. From 1996 to 2000, he trained to be a tool and die maker. Occasionally, he worked in the food service industry. In 2012, Güçyeter founded Elif Verlag, a publishing house focused on poetry, financed by his part-time job as a forklift driver. His latest poetry collection *Mein Prinz, ich bin das Ghetto* won the Peter Huchel Prize in 2022. His first novel, *Unser Deutschlandmärchen*, was published in the fall of 2022 by Mikrotext.

MATT GULLEY is a poet, playwright and fiction writer. He attended Wayne State University in Detroit and currently resides in Brooklyn with his partner Jenna. His work has appeared or is forthcoming in *Moon City Review, The Madrigal, The Minnesota Review* and *Consequence Forum.* Find him @selfawareroomba on Twitter or @mattgulley.bsky.social on Bluesky.

Primarily known for her melancholic, nostalgic, and brooding romantic poems that astutely reworked traditional styles and classical tropes to draw more attention to women's roles, KAROLINE VON GÜNDERRODE (1780-1806) is an important poet of the German tradition. However, amongst Anglophone readers she has not yet received the critical attention that she and her impressive poetic production deserve. A protofeminist author often writing under the pen name "Tian," Günderrode frequently turned her exacting eye to the disparity between genders, limiting societal strictures, and women's lack of autonomy and opportunity. She did so in her poems as well as in other writings of resistance and appraisal that denounced repressive traditional values.

YOLANDA HANSEN is an emerging poet lives and writes in Saskatchewan, Canada, where she works with the writing community and reads all she can get her hands on. Her work has appeared in *Briarpatch Magazine* and *Deep Wild Journal.*

ALANI ROSA HICKS-BARTLETT is a writer and translator who lives on the East Coast, where she finds herself increasingly in a nudiustertian mode. Her recent work has appeared in *Cagibi, ANMLY, carte blanche, The Stillwater Review, IthacaLit, Gathering Storm, Broad River Review, The Fourth River,* and *Mantis,* among others. She is currently working a collection of villanelles, and a translation of Medieval French poetry.

DAVID HARRISON HORTON is a Beijing-based writer, artist, editor and curator. He is author of Maze Poems (Arteidolia) and the chapbooks *Pete Hoffman Days* (Pinball) and *BeiHai* (Nanjing Poetry). He edits the poetry zine *SAGINAW.*

SHANE INGAN is from Indiana and lives in Detroit. Later this year, he will be releasing the first volume of a six-volume book of poetry titled *Vanity.*

Apart from being one of Holland's most important and widely awarded poets, ESTHER JANSMA is an influential archaeologist at the National Cultural Heritage Agency. Her poetry explores time and memory, death, legacy. It draws fresh power from these perennial themes because she often writes from two opposite and complementary viewpoints.

PARK JOON made his debut in 2008 through Silchon Munhak. His first poetry collection *I Took Your Name and Ate It for Some Days* was a bestseller that sold over 100,000 copies in South Korea alone, ranking ninth among bestselling poetry collections on Interpark Books for five years. He won the Park Jaesam Literature Award and the Pyeon-un Literature Award in 2019, and the Shin Dong-yup Prize for Literature in 2013. Apart from the two poetry collections, he has co-authored five different anthologies and published the essay collection *Though Crying Won't Change a Thing* that won the Prize for Young Artists.

SUSAN K received her BA in English Literature and Linguistics at the University of Toronto. She has completed the Literature Translation fellowship program and the Media Translation fellowship program at the Literature Translation Institute of Korea and currently works as a full-time freelance translator of Korean literature, web comics, films, and cultural contents into English. In 2021, she received two grants from the LTI to translate Korean poetry into English: Park Soran's *One Person's Closed Door* and Park Joon's *We Could See the Monsoon Together*. She translated Jeong Wooshin's poetry collection *I'll Give You All My Promenade* (Asia Publishers, 2022), and co-translated Kim Haengsook's *Human Time* (Black Ocean, 2023).

NINA KNUEVEN holds an MFA in poetry from Randolph College and was the Lead Poetry Editor at *Revolute*. Currently a fiction judge at NYC at Midnight, Knueven's work has appeared, or is forthcoming, in *The Ilanot Review*, *Gyroscope Review*, *The White Wall Review*, *Heavy Feather*, *River River*, and elsewhere. Knueven lives in Cincinnati with both human and animal family.

JAMES PH. KOTSYBAR, published in six countries, is the first poet (honored by NASA to be) published to another planet. His verse orbits Mars (at NASA's request and www voting), became part of Hubble Space Telescope's Mission Log, and was awarded and featured at NASA's Centaur's 50th Anniversary Art Challenge. Other honors include State Poetry Society of Michigan (awarded while Joseph Gordon-Levitt serendipitously workshopped this one-page poem into a short screenplay). He has read at the Los Angeles Performing Arts Center and for Troubadours, (Europe's oldest literary institution) in their founding city of Toulouse, France, at EuroScience Open Forum, Europe's largest interdisciplinary science event, earning a standing return invitation. He also once sang the poetry of William Blake with Allen Ginsberg at Santa Barbara's Old Vic Theater.

BEE LB is an array of letters, bound to impulse; a writer creating delicate connections. they have called any number of places home; currently, a single yellow wall in Michigan. they have been published in *FOLIO*, *Figure 1*, *The Offing*, and *Harpur Palate*, among others. their portfolio can be found at twinbrights.carrd.co

LINDA LEAVELL is the author of *Holding On Upside Down: The Life and Work of Marianne Moore* and of *Marianne Moore and the Visual Arts: Prismatic Color*. She is now working on a group biography of three photographers and four painters in the Stieglitz circle.

NAOMI BESS LEIMSIDER's poetry book, *Wild Evolution*, was published by Cathexis Northwest Press in June 2023. In addition, she has published poems, flash fiction, and short stories in numerous journals, including *Unleash Lit*, *Packingtown Review*, *Tangled Locks Journal*, *Booth*, *Anti-Heroin Chic*, *Wild Roof Journal*, *Syncopation Literary Journal*, *On the Seawall*, *Exquisite Pandemic*, *Orca*, *Hamilton Stone Review*, *Rogue Agent Journal*, *Newtown Literary*, *Otis Nebula*, *Quarterly West*, and *The Adirondack Review*. She has been a finalist for the Acacia Fiction Prize, the Saguaro Poetry Prize, and the Tiny Fork Chapbook Contest. In 2022, she received a Pushcart Prize nomination for fiction.

DOTTY LEMIEUX writes both poetry and poetic memoir. She has published five chapbooks, two during the pandemic: *Henceforth I Ask Not Good Fortune* in 2021, from Finishing Line Press and *Viruses, Guns and War* from Main Street Rag Press in 2023. Her work has appeared in numerous publications, such as *Rise Up Review*, *Wild Roof*, *MacQueen's Quinterly* and others. She has received one Best of the Net nomination.

KEVIN LEMASTER is the author of the chapbooks *Mercy* (Arroyo Seco Press, 2023) and *In The Throes Of Beauty* (forthcoming from

Finishing Line Press), and has been nominated twice for a Pushcart Prize twice and once for a Best of Net. Kevin has published poems in *Gyroscope Review*, *Hive Avenue Literary Journal*, *Main Street Rag*, *Barely South Review*, *Mantis*, *Amistad*, *SheilaNaGig online*, and has work forthcoming in *Chiron Review*, *Noctua Review*, *Landlocked*, *Rubbertop Review*, and others.

JAKE LEVINE is an assistant professor of Creative Writing at Keimyung University. He has written and translated or co-translated over a dozen books, including Kim Yideum's *Hysteria* (Action Books, 2019) which was the first book to be awarded both the National Translation Award and the Lucien Stryk Prize. He is a former Fulbright Fellow (to Lithuania in 2010), a recipient of a Korean Government Scholarship, served as an assistant editor at Acta Koreana, as a poetry editor at Spork Press, as the managing editor and editor-in-chief at *Sonora Review*, and currently edits the award-winning contemporary Korean poetry series, Moon Country, at Black Ocean. He has also translated other cultural contents such as Yun Hyong-Keun's diaries and narration for the K-pop group ENHYPEN. His first full-length book of poetry *The Imagined Country* was published by Tolsun Books in 2023.

MIA LINDENBURG is a writer based in the New York area, with a background in slam poetry. She focuses on written-word poetry about Seattle, mental health, and nostalgia. Outside of her work in poetry, she is a current graduate student at NYU, where she studies literature and library science.

CHRISTIAN LOPAC is a translator and holds an MA in religious studies from the University of Chicago. Lopac's translations of Bosnian poetry have appeared in *Delos* ("Six Bosnian Sevdalinka Songs").

KAREN LOZINSKI is a New York City native who lives in New Orleans. She's a writer, poet, artist, photographer, and musician who earned her MFA at the California Institute of the Arts. Her photographs and artwork have been in multiple shows and are widely published, and a selection of her music photos is included in *Can't Be Faded: Twenty Years in the New Orleans Brass Band Game* from the University of Mississippi Press. At work on a novel and poetry collection, her writing appears in *Talon Review*, *Scapegoat Review*,

Red Ogre Review, The Dead Mule School of Southern Literature, Red Noise Collective, and *Chapter House Journal,* and is forthcoming in *Defunkt, ellipsis… literature and art, The Citron Review,* and *300 Days of Sun.*

RICHIE MAGNIA is a student at the University of North Texas, studying Media Arts and Creative Writing. Focusing on topics such as boyhood, familial dynamics, and loss of innocence, he writes primarily in screenwriting, poetry, and short fiction. Richie is also the co-president and co-founder of UNT's Screenwriting Club. He can be found on Instagram @richiemagnia.

SAMANTHA MALAY's poetry recently appeared in *Kind Writers, Five South,* and *Plainsongs.* She grew up in rural northeastern Washington state, where her family built a cabin with timbers salvaged from an abandoned homestead, hauled water from a creek, and read by kerosene lamp. Her experiences in that time and place continue to shape her work. https://samanthamalay.com/

MARGARET MARCUM lives in Texas with her cats, Angel Clare, Alice, Adam, and Mazzy. She recently graduated from the MFA program in creative writing at Florida Atlantic University. Her poems have appeared in *Amethyst Review, Barzakh Magazine, Coffin Bell Journal, NonBinary Review, Scapegoat Review, The Islandia Journal, October Hill Magazine, Writing in a Woman's Voice,* and *Children, Churches, and Daddies,* among others.

J. PARKER MARVIN is currently a data analyst working in the semiconductor industry and lives in Saitama, Japan. Parker's poems have been published most recently in *Thin Air, Levitate,* and *Second Factory.* Parker's collection *Postlude to the End of* is forthcoming in the Fall of 2024 from April Gloaming.

RILEY MAYES is a poet and creative nonfiction writer from Portland, Maine. She is currently pursuing her MSc in Literature from the University of Edinburgh, where she lives with her partner, sometimes her neighbour's cats, and hundreds of books. Her work has been featured in several publications, including *Anthroposhere: Oxford Climate Review, River and South Review, New Note Poetry,* and *Route 7 Review.*

CRISTANNE MILLER is SUNY Distinguished Professor and Edward H. Butler Professor of English at the University at Buffalo SUNY. She has published broadly on nineteenth- and twentieth-century poetry. On Moore, her books include *Marianne Moore: Questions of Authority* (1995); *Cultures of Modernism: Marianne Moore, Mina Loy, Else Lasker-Schüler. Gender and Literary Community in New York and Berlin* (2005); and *The Selected Letters of Marianne Moore* (1997; General Editor: Bonnie Costello). Miller is also founder and director of the *Marianne Moore Digital Archive*—an electronic archive that is publishing in digitized, transcribed, and annotated form all 122 of Moore's working notebooks. On Dickinson, Miller has published three monographs and edited Emily Dickinson's *Poems: As She Preserved Them* (2016), winner of the MLA Best Scholarly Edition Prize, and *The Letters of Emily Dickinson* (co-edited with Domhnall Mitchell, 2024).

BOBBY MORRIS (he/him) is a Filipino-American student, poet, and educator in Nevada. He loves when his own creation argues with him and play with his ear. You can find more of his work on his website: bobbymorris.net.

Author of "Journeyed Marks of a Vague Land", YAKOUB MOUSLI is an Algerian writer and poet whose works, including books, poems and short stories, have been published internationally; featuring in several anthologies and literary journals such as *Cardinal Sins* and *Poets' Choice*.

WILL NEUENFELDT (he/him) studied English at Gustavus Adolphus College and his poems are published in *Capsule Stories*, *Months to Years*, and *Red Flag Poetry*. He lives in Cottage Grove, MN, home of the dude who played Steven Stifler in those American Pie movies and a house Teddy Roosevelt slept in. Instagram.com/wjnpoems.

LINA ODEH, a 25-year-old writer and scholar based at Tel Aviv University, hailing from Nazareth, explores themes of romance and coming of age in her poetry. Her debut poems appeared in Caesura, Tel Aviv University's poetry journal, in 2023, where she later became an editor. Intrigued by the interplay of form, content, and their ties to the concrete life and one's spiritual experience, she delves into their nuanced relationship in her work.

FERNANDO MARTINEZ PERISET is a PhD student in the department of Comparative Literature at Stanford University. Before joining Stanford, he studied in the UK, France and Ireland. His interests include Early Modern studies, intellectual history, the history of emotions... and petting cute cats!

CAROLINE WILCOX REUL is the translator of *In the morning we are glass*, by Andra Schwarz (Zephyr Press, 2021) and *Who Lives by Elisabeth Borchers* (Tavern Books, 2017), both from the German. Her translations have appeared or are forthcoming in the *PEN Poetry Series*, *The Los Angeles Review*, *Waxwing*, *The Michigan Quarterly Review*, *The Columbia Journal*, *ANMLY*, the *Arkansas International*, and others.

DAVID ROMANDA's work has appeared in places such as *Columbia Review*, *The Louisville Review*, and *Puerto del Sol*. His book is *Why Does She Always Talk About Her Husband?* (Blue Cedar Press, 2022). Romanda lives in Kawasaki City, Japan.

RSVP is working on his 3rd unpublished collection of 30 years of poetry in excess. *From Here To There*, is entirely written in the past year (May 2023-24) in Taiwan, where he resides. He was born in Brooklyn, NYC, lived also in Harlem (before leaving for South Asia), Miami (Florida, and many other cities there), Boston, MA (for 8 yrs, 3 mths, & 12 days), and other memorable places. Reginald Saint-Vincent Paul's *Mirror-Mirror*, is his reflection on his ways, of living in ecstasy, w/o shame, nor limits.

FERESHTEH SARI (born 1956) is a writer, editor, and Russian translator who began her writing career in the 1980s by publishing her first collection of poetry, *Echoes of Silence*. She is the author of eight books of poetry, six novels, and several children's and young adult books. She was awarded the Hellman/Hammett Grant in 1998 and won Iran's prestigious poetry award, the Parvin Etesami Prize, in 2004 for her poetry collection *Days and Letters*. She lives in Tehran, Iran.

PARISA SARANJ is a writer, translator, and editor at Consequence Forum. Her writings on contemporary Iranian politics and translations from Persian have been published in several online and print publications, including *Ms. Magazine*, *Defunct*, *Two Lines*, *Your Impossible Voice*, and *Green Linden Tree*. She has also translated two documentaries on women's rights in Iran, *Nasrin* (2020) and *Sansur* (2023).

WHITNEY SCHMIDT is a teacher, writer, and amateur lepidopterist with a passion for poetry and pollinators. She founded the first student-led secondary school Writing Center in Oklahoma and co-sponsors her school's LGBTQIA+ affinity group. Her work has appeared or is forthcoming in *Harbinger, So to Speak, Wingless Dreamer,* and *Wild Roof Journal.* She lives near Tulsa with her husband, two pit-mix pups, and various moth and butterfly guests.

T.W. SIA (he/him) is a queer immigrant from Myanmar. He holds a BA from Swarthmore College and is pursuing an MD from Stanford University. He writes poetry to study and practice a different medium of healing. His most recent poems have been published by *TAB Journal, Mud Season Review,* and elsewhere.

MAZZY SLEEP is a 12-year-old from Toronto, Canada. She has written over a thousand poems and short stories, as well as three novels and two feature screenplays. Her work has appeared in *Blackbird, The Margins* (Asian American Writers' Workshop), *The Minnesota Review, Rattle, Barren Magazine, Geist, Maudlin House,* and elsewhere. Mazzy was commissioned by the Lunar Codex project to write a poem that landed on the moon in February 2024. She was also commended by 2021 T.S. Eliot Prize winner Joelle Taylor in the Waltham Forest Poetry Competition. mazzysleep.com.

HELEN STEENHUIS, originally from Atlanta, Georgia, has been living in France near Aix-en-Provence for 35 years. She is an English language teacher, raises chickens, and swims in the Mediterranean year long. Her work has appeared in the *French Literary Review, Equinox, The Poetry Library,* and *Cumberland River Review.* Recent poems are forthcoming in *Amethyst Review,* and *Kitchen Table Quarterly.*

ROWAN TATE is an emerging Romanian songwriter, poet, and tree whisperer. Her work is visually fervent and deeply felt. She reads nonfiction nature books, the backs of shampoo bottles, and sometimes minds.

SOPHIA TERAZAWA is the author of three collections, *Winter Phoenix* (Deep Vellum, 2021), *Anon* (Deep Vellum, 2023), and the forthcoming *Oracular Maladies*, a finalist for the 2023 Noemi Press Book Award. She has also published two chapbooks, *I AM NOT A WAR* (Essay Press, 2016) and *Correspondent Medley* (Factory Hollow Press, 2019), winner of the 2018 Tomaž Šalamun Prize. She currently teaches poetry at Virginia Tech as Visiting Assistant Professor. Her debut novel is forthcoming with A Strange Object in 2025.

T.M. THOMSON is co-author of *Frame & Mount the Sky* (2017), a chapbook of ekphrastic poetry, as well the author as *Strum and Lull* (2019) and *The Profusion* (2019). She is a lover of animals, art, trees, surrealism, black and white movies, walking in autumn rains, feeding wild birds in winter, playing in spring mud, & bat-watching in summer. Her first full-length collection of poems, *Plunge*, has just been published by Uncollected Press.

TJIZEMBUA TJIKUZU is an essayist and poet from Aminuis, Namibia. He graduated from the Rutgers-Camden MFA in Creative Writing program in 2021. He has poetry and essays published and forthcoming in *Doek! Literary Magazine, Obsidian Literature and Arts in the African Diaspora, Rigorous Magazine, Empyrean Literary Magazine, Columbia: Journal of Literature and Art, Consequence Forum, Tint Journal, The Elevation Review, Barely South Review*, and *Santa Fe Literary Review*. He currently lives in Philadelphia, PA.

ABHISHEK UDAYKUMAR is a writer, filmmaker and painter from India. He graduated from Royal Holloway University of London with English and Creative Writing. His narratives reflect the human condition of rural and urban worlds, and explore eternal landscapes through film and prose. He is passionate about old-school illustrations, Persian Miniatures, *qawwali* music, carnivalesque tales and marine life; and reading Tamil, Hindi and Urdu. He has been published by different literary journals and has made thirteen independent films. He hopes to live in a cabin amongst tree overlords and joyous amphibians.

B.A. VAN SISE is an author and photographic artist focused on the intersection between language and the visual image. He is the author of three monographs: the visual poetry anthology *Children of Grass: A Portrait of American Poetry, Invited to Life: After the Holocaust,* and the upcoming *On the National Language: The Poetry of America's Endangered Tongues.* He has previously been featured in solo exhibitions at the Center for Creative Photography, the Woody Guthrie Center, the Rockefeller Arts Center, the Center for Jewish History and the Museum of Jewish Heritage. He has been a finalist for the *Rattle* Poetry Prize, the Travel Media Awards for feature writing, and the Meitar Award for Excellence in Photography. He is a 2022 New York State Council on the Arts Fellow in Photography, a Phillip and Edith Leonian Foundation grant recipient, a Prix de la Photographie Paris award-winner, a winner of the Colonel Darron L. Wright Memorial Writing Awards and the Lascaux Prize for Nonfiction, and an Independent Book Publishers Awards gold medalist. The son of an Italian mother of Tunisian and Libyan descent, he lives in New York City.

M. VASALIS (Margaretha Leenmans) is one of the all-time favorite poets in The Netherlands, winning the most prestigious P.C.Hooft Oeuvre Prize – awarded only once in 3 years. For most of her professional life she was also a children's psychiatrist. Her 1000-page biography is a national treasure.

A long-time poet, ELAINE VERDILL is also a photographer and painter. Her writings can be found in such publications as *The Bookends Review*, *Plainsongs*, *American Chordata*, *Minerva Rising Press*, and *Claudius Speaks*.

BERNARDO VILLELA has had poetry published by *Entropy*, *Zoetic Press*, and *Bluepepper and Eldritch & Ether*; and poetry translations in *New Delta Review* and *AzonaL*. You can read more about these and various other pursuits at https://linktr.ee/bernardovillela.

MARISA VITO is a queer Californian, Filipinx poet who has published with *Crab Fat Magazine*, *The Spectacle*, *Mixed Mag*, *Phyll Magazine*, and the *Los Angeles Magazine*. They graduated from the University of California, San Diego with a degree in English Literature/Writing and are currently the Digital Content Manager for Copper Canyon Press. When not reading or writing, they enjoy cooking, baking, gardening, and studying/talking about societal theory. They are based in Brooklyn, NY.

MOIRA WALSH is the author of *Earthrise* (Penteract Press, 2023) and, with Wilfried Schubert, *Do Try This at Home* (Animal Heart Press, 2024). Her poetry can be found in *Bennington Review*, *Denver Quarterly*, *Poetry Northwest*, and other fine places. A founding member of Kollektief Dellgart, Moira has co-translated work by contemporary poets Olja Alvir, Ken Mikolowski, Mariia Mykytsei, Halyna Petrosaniak, and Maë Schwinghammer.

J. CATCHER WARD is a writer at large in the world.

SPENCER JAYU WARD is a Korean American hapa, poet, policy wonk, and ADHDer who wears too many hats. A Seattle local who began writing poetry in high school, he has a B.A. in International Affairs and Economics from the University of Washington, where he specialized in diplomacy and nuclear nonproliferation. After cutting his teeth as a policy research writer and editor at legislative offices and nonprofits in Washington, D.C., he settled back home, and now helps students with disabilities of all ages as a high school behavioral therapist and language arts tutor.

SHAO WEI grew up with her grandfather by the Yangtze River in China and came to the United States in 1996. She earned a MA in Creative Writing from New York University, a MFA from the Michener Center for Writers at UT Austin, Ph.D. in from UT Dallas. Her books include *Pulling A Dragon's Teeth* (Pitts Press) and a memoir, *Homeland* (Taipei).

JENNIFER WEIGEL is a multi-disciplinary mixed media conceptual artist. Weigel utilizes a wide range of media to convey her ideas, including assemblage, drawing, fibers, installation, jewelry, painting, performance, photography, sculpture, video and writing. Much of her work touches on themes of beauty, identity (especially gender identity), memory & forgetting, and institutional critique. You can read more of Weigel's writing on her website here. https://jenniferweigelwords.wordpress.com/

Six times nominated for a Pushcart, once for Best of the Net, FLORENCE WEINBERGER is the author of six books of poetry, most recently These Days of Simple Mooring, winner of the Blue Light Press Book Award. Her poems have appeared in journals including *Calyx, Rattle, Mantis, Miramar, River Styx, Ellipsis, Poet Lore, Comstock Review, Baltimore Review, Nimrod, Cider Press Review, Poetry East, Shenandoah*, and numerous anthologies.

NICHOLAS WONG is a poet, translator and visual artist from Hong Kong. He is the author of *Crevasse*, winner of the Lambda

Literary Awards in Gay Poetry, and *Besiege Me*, also a Lammy finalist in the same category. His poems and translations are forthcoming in *The Georgia Review*, *Epiphany*, *fourteen poems*, *The Massachusetts Review*, and *The Griffith Review*. IG: citiesofsameness.

XIAOQIU is a Chinese poet and translator. He is an editor at *Interim* magazine and recently put together a special issue of translation on the theme of "Carrying Over". His award-winning work has been published in *Meridian*, *Reed Magazine*, *Sunspot Lit*, and more. His translated poems have been published by *Lunch Ticket*, *ANTONYM*, and *DEFUNCT*. His poetry chapbook *Other Side of Sea* has been published by Etchings Press by the University of Indianapolis. He translates from the Chinese and Spanish. Currently, he is a Black Mountain Institute Fellow and a PhD student of Creative Writing at UNLV.

KENTON K. YEE's recent poems appear (or will soon) in *Plume Poetry*, *Threepenny Review*, *TAB Journal*, *I-70 Review*, *Hawaii Pacific Review*, *Terrain.org*, *Mantis*, *McNeese Review*, *Indianapolis Review*, and *Rattle*, among others. A Stanford alumnus (MA '00, JD '00, and PhD '01), Kenton taught at Columbia University and writes and consults in the San Francisco Bay Area.

JAKE ZAWLACKI is a writer, translator, and scholar. He holds a master's degree in Russian, Eastern European and Eurasian Studies from Stanford University and an MFA from Louisiana State University. He has been the recipient of a Fulbright Fellowship to the Kyrgyz Republic and has written scholarly works on Kazakh animation and folklore, and Kyrgyz traditional health practices. His creative work often explores meaning and free will through experimental and metafictional forms and can be found at *The Saturday Evening Post*, *The Journal*, and *The Citron Review*. Additional translations of Akhmet Baitursynuly's work have been published in *Asymptote* and *Guernica*.

Printed in the USA
CPSIA information can be obtained
at www.ICGtesting.com
LVHW052329200924
791669LV00010B/93